BOOKS BY FRANK S. SMYTHE

THE SPIRIT OF THE HILLS

" Mr. Smythe is a distinguished mountaineer. He has a genuine love of the mountains. . . . He has a natural gift of eloquence, and a power of rapid narrative."—THE TIMES.

CAMP SIX

" It would be hard to imagine a better man than Mr. Smythe to write such a book. . . . His high altitude writing is pure gold."—DAILY TELEGRAPH.

OVER TYROLESE HILLS

" British mountaineers are proud of Mr. Frank Smythe. . . . His book brings the very air and sun of the mountains into the reader's room. It has the touch of a master mountaineer."—E. F. BOZMAN, OBSERVER.

MOUNTAINEERING HOLIDAY

" Mr. Smythe adds to his achievements as a mountaineer the ability to write graphically and gracefully about mountains with really remarkable skill."—MANCHESTER GUARDIAN.

THE VALLEY OF FLOWERS

·" The snows and the flowers lie cheek by jowl ; one can be a mountaineer in the morning, a gardener in the afternoon, and a dazzled dreamer by the night's camp fire." —THE TIMES LITERARY SUPPLEMENT.

KAMET CONQUERED

" To read this book is to surmise that in years to come this ascent of Kamet will be considered one of the decisive climbs in the history of mountaineering."—THE TIMES LITERARY SUPPLEMENT.

ALPINE JOURNEY

" Never in my life have I spent six such delightful weeks in the Alps."—FRANK S. SMYTHE.

MOUNTAIN VISION

This is Frank Smythe's very newest book— a magnificent companion to " The Spirit of the Hills."

EDWARD WHYMPER

" Will become a classic . . . there are two souls in this book, Smythe's as well as Whymper's." —OBSERVER.

THE ROUTE TAKEN OVER MONT BLANC

Stanford, London.

Miles

Aiguille Géant
Aiguille du Géant
TORINO HUT
AIGUILLE DE LA BRENVA
Col de la Fourche
La Tour Ronde
Aiguille de la Brenva
Mt Blanc du Tacul
GLACIER DE LA BRENVA
Aiguille Noire de Peuterey
P. Durier
Mt Maudit
Col de la Brenva
GLACIER DI FRENEY
To Chamonix
Aiguille du Gouter
Dôme du Gouter
14,120 FT
Vallot Hut 14,310 FT
Les Bosses
Col de Bionnassay
MONT BLANC 15,780 FT
Mt Blanco di Courmayeur
GLACIER DEL BROILLA
M. Vorassay
To St Gervais-les-Bains
GL. DE BIONNASSAY
Aiguille de Bionnassay 13,295 FT
G. Sella
GLACIER DI MIAGE
Gonella Hut
GL. DEL DOME
GLACIER DEL MT BLANCO
GL. DI BIONNASSAY
Aiguille de Trélatête
Col de Miage Dorier Hut
Col de Miage 11,015 FT
GL. DE LA FRASSE
Dôme de Miage
Petit Mt Blanc
Aiguille de Béranger
GL. DE TRÉLATÊTE
To Trélatête Hotel
Aiguille de Trélatête
Val Veni
Edora di Veni

FRANK S. SMYTHE

MOUNTAINEERING HOLIDAY

HODDER AND STOUGHTON
ST. PAUL'S HOUSE, LONDON, E.C.4

First Printed *1940*
Second Edition (*First in this form*) . *May 1941*

Made and Printed in Great Britain for Hodder and Stoughton Limited,
by Butler and Tanner Ltd., Frome and London

TO
JIM

CONTENTS

CONTENTS

ILLUSTRATIONS

CHAPTER I

TO THE ALPS

THERE is no holiday like a mountaineering holiday. For eleven months the mountaineer has lived, perhaps in a city, perhaps amidst fields and hedges, on ground tamed, cultivated, and built upon by the hand of man; and he has sighed for a glimpse of mountains, for the mountain wind on his cheek, keen, pure, and cold, for the lilt of the mountain stream, for the feel of rock in his hand, for the crunch of frozen snow beneath his feet, for the smell of mist and the fragrance of alp and pine forest.

In his spare moments he has read about mountains, pored over maps, and studied guide-books. Then comes the day when he inspects his boots, his ice axe, and his rope. He packs his suitcase and his rucksack. He buys his railway ticket. The incredible has become credible. For two weeks, three weeks, or a month he will escape from civilisation and all its works; he is off to the mountains.

Jim Gavin and I met at Victoria Station on the afternoon of July 29th, 1939. The rush to the Continent was at its height, and the platform was crowded with holiday-makers. I remember that, as I stood watching the bustle, I longed for the quiet silent places, where I should not have to listen to the explosions of the internal combustion engine, breathe the sickly fumes of petrol, jostle my way along crowded pavements, eat in the glare of electric light, wake up to an array of chimney-pots crouched beneath a looming pall of smoke.

A boat train is an interesting spectacle, collectively and individually. Many curious types and conditions of English people venture abroad for their holidays. Gentlemen, who normally only wear plus-fours when playing golf, feel compelled to don them when visiting the Continent. Perhaps they want the foreigner to recognise them as Englishmen, and the foreigner, be he Frenchman or German, Turk or Italian, welcomes them. He knows instinctively, and from long experience, that they may be imposed upon in all manner of ways. In the tourist business the plus-foured Englishman is a palpable means of wealth.

Then there is the hiker who dresses himself in his oldest, shabbiest, and dirtiest clothes. He will be seen any day during the tourist season at Victoria attired in a pair of filthy shorts or stained flannel trousers, an open-necked shirt, and a tattered sports coat. On his legs are a pair of gaudily-topped stockings, on his feet a pair of clumping boots, and on his head a felt hat, the appearance of which suggests that it has been previously kicked for some miles through the streets of London. Lastly, on his back is an enormous rucksack, which in age, condition, and appearance matches itself perfectly with the items already described. Further to prepare for his Continental holiday, he has omitted to shave for the past few days.

Certain questions inevitably occur. Why is it necessary for him to start his holiday in this condition? What will be his appearance at the end of the holiday, and what will be the reactions of those among whom he spends his holiday? Is it his intention to impress the foreigner by the "toughness" of his demeanour and appearance, or is it simply a manifestation of the Englishman's innate love of hard living, open air, cold baths, roast beef, etc. etc.?

Then there is, I regret to state, a certain type of mountaineer, whose objects appear similar to those of the hiker. He is wreathed around with ropes; crampons and ice axes radiate from him at uncomfortable and dangerous angles; his boots, armoured with sharp saw-edged nails, are a source of constant anxiety to others less heavily shod in passport and customs queues, and a perpetual menace to parquet and polished floors. His clothing exudes a peculiar stale, musty odour. He has a lofty and superior mien, and looks superciliously at those not similarly attired and equipped, as much as to say: "I am better than you. I am tough, a he-man. Look at my rope, my ice axe, my boots. I am a mountaineer; as for you, you are kittle-kattle, mere tourists."

These strange personages are happily in a minority, if a very evident minority. The majority of the travellers consists of ordinary tourists. Some of these would not like to be described thus, for they are bound for places, expensive places, where ordinary tourists do not congregate. They are select, well groomed, languid, and they exude, in contrast to the mountaineer already mentioned, expensive perfumes. They are experienced travellers, and one feels instinctively that the hotel labels on their luggage are genuine, and not purchased as a mixed bag in Paris.

3

Then there are the genuine tourists, those incapable of fending for themselves, the products of Messrs Cook, Lunn, Frame, and other agencies. Their centre of gravity is a courier, a harassed, nervous person usually to be seen hurrying about with folios of tickets in his hand, whose life is spent in constant fear lest something go wrong, whose mind is a sort of perpetual motion machine of time-tables, reservations, passports, and landing tickets. It is interesting to speculate as to what would happen to his flock were he to be taken ill, fall overboard, go on strike, die, or, simply, to vanish.

Off at last! Waving hands and a flutter of handkerchiefs, a last barrage of kisses, and the packed train steals out from beneath the grim, smoke-grimed vault of Victoria. The holiday has begun.

The train does not get very far. After labouring heavily for some ten minutes it comes to a halt in a suburb of London. There it waits for five minutes, then continues for a short distance, only to come to another halt in another suburb. We remember that we are on the Southern Railway and take stock of our surroundings.

The foreigner's first entry into London must be a depressing experience. He sees suburbia, an expanse as monotonous as any desert, but without a desert's charms of distance and serenity. As Karel Capek wrote in *Letters from England*: "The train flies past a whole town which is beset by some terrible curse; inexorable Fate has decreed that each house shall have two pillars at the door. For another huge block, she has decreed iron balconies. The following block she has perpetually condemned to grey

4

brick. On another mournful street she has relentlessly imposed blue verandahs. Then there is a whole quarter doing penance for some unknown wrong by placing five steps before every front door. I should be enormously relieved if even one house had only three."

Yet if Fate has condemned man to be the slave of outward appearance, signs of diverseness in his character and intellect are discernible in the gardens that adjoin the railway. Some are desolate wastes in which dustbins stand in sordid repose, and a few blades of grass eke out a grimy and a precarious existence, but others bear evidence of his struggle to preserve a feeling for beauty amid the uglinesses of his own construction, and cheek by jowl with a patch, containing nothing more exciting or original than a few cabbages blackened by the smoke and soot of passing trains, exists a well-tended lawn, with perhaps a surround of flower-beds together with one or two shrubs, a sundial, a bird-bath, and a tiny greenhouse.

High up on the embankment, the passer-by looks down dispassionately on this evidence of human activity. He may feel sad or glad according to his mood, but for the most part he will gaze unseeing, for suburbia has come to be an accepted part of the twentieth-century system. Yet the struggle goes on. Every flower that is planted in these little gardens is indicative of some flicker, some spark to set the human soul afire.

The countryside, when at last the train has struggled through the suburbs, inspires altogether different reflections. Foreigners regard it with horror. "Why," they say, "in our country this would be cultivated. Here it is mostly going to waste." And they gaze from the windows of the train at the broad acres of Kent as though at a criminal who stands morally and socially condemned. To such outspoken condemnation, the Englishman replies lamely that industrialisation is responsible and that the yeomen of England have gravitated to the towns. He goes on to explain that it is cheaper to import butter, eggs, and bacon from Denmark and Holland, meat from New Zealand and the Argentine, that farming doesn't pay, that agricultural wages are too high to make it pay, and so on and so forth. To all this the foreigner listens politely but without much attention. His eyes are fixed on the fields that flash by, upon the derelict-looking farms, upon tracts of coarse sedge grass and deserted grazing-land.

"But you could be self-supporting if you cultivated this. In my country . . ."

Sevenoaks marks the limit of suburbia, though some would maintain that Tonbridge is now within the grip of Greater London. Beyond Tonbridge there is indisputably country. When I was a child I lived near the railway between Tonbridge and Paddock Wood, and the Continental expresses held an irresistible fascination for me. I used to ask myself whether I should ever travel in one and cross the sea to a new land.

For a few instants I saw the house where I lived between the trees. The trees were a little higher, but the house was unchanged, and so were the oast-houses beyond it. Here I was, *en route* to the Continent and the Alps. I was thirty-nine years of age, but for a split second

I lay again on the same daisy-sprinkled bank, my chin cupped in my hands, and watched the Continental express roar past towards new lands.

Marden, Staplehurst, Headcorn, Pluckley—these are sleepy little villages on a long straight stretch of railway between Tonbridge and Ashford, where engine-drivers of Continental expresses do their best to make up for lost time. They do not appear to have changed, nor does the Weald of Kent. The fields, the copses, the woods, the oast-houses are much the same as they used to be, and in the north beyond the Weald loom hills in the same blue line. This is the real England; this England changes little; this England is not concerned with a hurrying industrialism; it is slow, and essentially conservative; in this lies its strength, its beauty, and its happiness. If you were called upon to think of some scene, some vista typical of England, of what would you think, what picture would form in your mind? I have sometimes asked myself this and the answer is always the same. It is a simple English countryside, the countryside seen from the window of any train. I come from Kent, and I think of the Kentish countryside. For all the aeroplanes that drone overhead, the motors that rush along the roads, it is very peaceful. It calls to mind the pealing of church bells through a still air, the rushing of water over a mill-stream sluice, a chorus of rooks from tall elms, the scent of new-mown hay, and freshly gathered hops.

Through such memories men best discern the meaning and the value of their native land. The English tradition lies not in towns, coal-mines, and factories, but in fields, hedges, woods, and slow-running streams; in mellowed bricks and ivy; in tall trees and smooth green lawns; in smoke-blue distances and soft grey skies.

Beyond Ashford, through which the train jolts at high speed with a tirade of wailing and whistling, the character of the country changes. For a few miles it is undulating and wooded, then, suddenly, like a single bold stroke of a pen, come the South Downs. Here is something different from the trim and fertile Weald. The latter is circumscribed by hedges, fields, ditches, and roads, the former knows no such restrictions or limitations. The Downs are not mere earthy undulations, they are hills. They inherit the same freedom as the sea, the freedom of wind, storm, and sunshine, and they share with the sea an uncompromising simplicity of design. The face of the Weald changes according to the whims and fancies of man, but the Downs remain aloof and uncultivated, and because of this changelessness they epitomise the spirit of the past. In the Weald a man may escape back into the Middle Ages, but in a fold of the Downs he can travel farther than this; he can hear the tramp of Roman legions and the twanging of Saxon bow-strings, and he will feel deep down within him a heritage of hard-won experience, a pride, a solemnity, and a tradition.

The train passes between the shoulders of the Downs and the house-tops of Folkestone come into view, rows and rows of them slated and grey, with a single hideous gasometer brooding over them like some Cyclopian pill-box. Beyond the houses is the quivering glint of the sea.

When an Englishman is safely back in England from

the Continent and the horrors of the Channel crossing are forgotten, he will exclaim, "Thank God for the Channel!" In crossing that twenty miles of water he may lose the contents of his stomach but he will gain a wonderful feeling of security. When leaving England the sensation is different. Though he be under the aegis of Thomas Cook & Sons with his fare paid from beginning to end (including tips), he becomes an adventurer. For a few days or weeks England will know him not. He will see no English policeman; he will drink no English beer; he will eat no English beef; he will not hear "Paridowner-carplee" and other English sounds.

Between Folkestone and Dover it is possible to examine the state of the sea and estimate the chances of internal survival. On the present occasion they seemed excellent. Only the gentlest of waves lapped the chalk cliffs and the Channel stretched level and unheaving beneath a sky of pale hazy blue. As we emerged from the last tunnel Dover's stately castle came into view frowning down on the mean, ugly little town at its feet.

In another minute we arrived at the harbour station. The porters here are for the most part taciturn, grim-visaged men. Doubtless they have much to endure at the hands of excitable foreigners with a limited command of the English language. Having exchanged our luggage for a numbered token we took our places in the passport queue. Many uncomplimentary things, some deserved and some undeserved, have been written, and will yet be written, about the passport and customs arrangements at Folkestone and Dover. I have stood in the same puddle of water described by one infuriated writer to *The Times*; on the other hand, I have found the customs officials invariably courteous and scrupulously fair. For some reason they always seem to believe me, and I can only suppose that this is because I always tell them the truth. On one occasion only have I experienced trouble and that was when I forgot to declare an article of silk because I had forgotten its existence. The manner in which the officer divined that I had got such an article and ferreted it out, had in it more than an element of the occult. There is, however, the story of the old gentleman in the top hat. One day a stately old gentleman attired in a frock-coat, and an unusually tall and glossy silk hat, presented himself at the customs. His luggage was duly examined and found to be devoid of dutiable articles. The examining officer's attention was then drawn to the unusual size of the silk hat.

"Would you mind removing your hat, sir?" he asked.

At once the old gentleman bridled up.

"Certainly not," he replied. "What nonsense! I refuse to do any such thing."

This naturally aroused the official's suspicion and he said:

"I'm sorry, sir, but I must insist that you remove your hat."

"I will do no such thing," returned the old gentleman angrily.

This put the customs official in a quandary and he went off in search of a higher authority. In the end, the old gentleman was taken to the Chief Customs Officer, but declined as resolutely as before to remove his hat, and to the threat that it would be taken off by force replied that to do so would be an assault on his person. Finally, a police warrant was procured and the hat removed. There was nothing inside it. After that, there was, of course, a blazing row. The police blamed the Chief Customs Officer, and the Chief Customs Officer blamed his underling. After that, at odd intervals, the old gentleman used to be seen attired as usual in his frock-coat and tall silk hat. He became quite a well-known figure and none of the customs officials had the temerity to ask him to remove his hat a second time. One day, however, there was appointed a new junior customs official, a short-tempered and abrupt young man. To him the old gentleman presented himself, and to his intense astonishment was asked for the second time to remove his hat. He was even more indignant than on the previous occasion and worse than that, he was rude, very rude.

His rudeness was too much for the customs official. He was short-tempered himself, and he had had a trying day. Leaning across the counter, he deliberately knocked the silk hat from the old gentleman's head. It was packed with drugs.

Passengers often complain bitterly of queues. A voluntary queue is distasteful to most free-born Englishmen, but to be compulsorily herded is peculiarly galling. The young men who examine passports at Dover are as efficient as they are nonchalant. One flicks open the document and takes a peep, then passes it to another who takes another peep, shuts it up and hands it to the owner.

In addition, there are sometimes to be seen men in Burberrys whose sinister and watchful mien indubitably classes them as detectives.

If I were a spy I should write my notes on the pages of my passport. As it is, I reserve these pages for the names and addresses of people I meet on my travels, hotels, prices, rates of exchange, notes on wines and eatables, mountaineering details, articles to be purchased, etc. etc. Only once have the defaced pages aroused suspicion in the foreign breast and that, of course, was in Italy where everything unorthodox is suspicious to the Fascist ear or eye.

The voyage was uneventful. I am bound to admit that on the whole the Channel has been kind to me, but there have been times when it has not. I have tried most of the seasick remedies. One preventative of seasickness is to get thoroughly drunk, taking care, however, not to mix the drinks. Another effective method is to get a friend to knock you on the head at the commencement of the voyage. A third, and infallible, cure is to tie a handkerchief round the neck, insert a walking-stick, and twist.

The English Channel is no respecter of persons. A friend of mine was once crossing it on a very rough day. He is one of those disgusting fellows who strolls about smoking a large cigar when everyone else is wishing that he was dead. As he was promenading the deck, he espied a small man with a very green face huddled in a corner. My friend recognised him, and going up to him exclaimed with horrible heartiness: "Hullo, Admiral, what are you doing here?" The Admiral, for such indeed he was, gave a gulp, looked up, recognised my friend, and whispered, "For God's sake, don't call me Admiral here."

When the Channel is smooth I am glad to have been born an Englishman. I promenade the deck, thinking of tall ships, Nelson, and our heritage the sea. I look at the receding cliffs of Dover and thrill with patriotic pride and insular superiority. But when the sea is rough, I wish I had been born in Switzerland or Tibet, and creep away into a corner vainly hoping for a swift and merciful death.

To outward appearance Calais is no more exciting than Dover. However, the trains run about the streets in a most intriguing manner and the railway porters carry loads which would make a British railway porter shudder. It is apparent also to the traveller that he has set foot on the Continent because of the tendency to wear uniforms. No longer is he in an atmosphere of nondescript shop-keeping. He has entered the zone of efficient militarism, even though it is a democratic, and therefore benevolent, brand.

French customs officials are as courteous as British customs officials. Nevertheless, they have their foibles and weaknesses. At Dover, scents and cameras are greeted with hostility and suspicion, but at Calais and other French ports, an object of far less value titivates the official zeal and rouses the Gallic passion. New clothes, cameras, films, whisky, poufft!—they are nothing; half a pound of tobacco is dismissed with a wave of the hand; but stay! What is this? Yes, it is, incredible, unbelievable, a packet of one dozen boxes of matches, costing eightpence at the local grocer's. Alack and alas, it is borne off in triumph. Sadly we realise that we shall never see it again. In future, we must light our pipes and cigarettes with French matches. If we are lucky we get matches which when struck merely project molten sparks into the eyes. Remember, therefore, always to close the eyes when striking French matches. But if we are unlucky, we get matches which exude horrible sulphur fumes for some fifteen or twenty seconds, matches that in South America are called "Stinkerados" and not without reason. Matches are the price the English pipe-smoker must pay for a holiday in France. It would appear that the whole vigilance of the French customs is directed in a never-ending search for matches. Bold and fortunate indeed is he who can smuggle a few boxes past them, and in particular, past the women examiners whose whole feminine acuteness and perception seem to be directed in search of matches.

Nothing here need be written about French railway trains, except to state that they are bigger, more comfortable, more efficiently heated, and are said to have more accidents than English railway trains. Notices on them are presented to the traveller in three languages, not including English, and the schoolboy translation of the most prominent of these is: "It arrives frequently that the agents travelling on the line are blessed by bottles or other objects solid."

A French line "talks" differently to an English line. The English line says, "Rumpety-rump, rumpety-rump" in a slow traditional English way; the French line says, "Rumpty, rumpty, rumpty, rumpty" in a hurried, im-

patient manner. The French countryside between Calais
and Paris is altogether more spacious and more sensible
from an agricultural point of view than the English
countryside between Dover and London. The plough-
man does not have to about turn so frequently, and can
make a furrow half a mile or more in length. Also, of
course, more land is under cultivation. It tells, as elo-
quently as any countryside can tell, of a thrifty, hard-
working people, a people who do not play at farming
as a side-line to industry, but whose life and livelihood
are linked with the soil. Human efficiency, however,
seldom spells beauty when applied to Nature, and it is
natural for the Englishman to prefer his own countryside
of useless acres and hedges behind which he revels in his
privacy. Yet this countryside of northern France possesses
a grandeur, a beauty, and a dignity. It is just such a
countryside as Constable loved to paint, rolling in long
undulations, with wide horizons, blue distances, and
towering, slow-strolling clouds.

Paris is in odd contrast to the French countryside. If it
were representative of France as a whole it would be
spacious, staid, and dignified. It would go to bed early,
get up early, and be thrifty and hard-working. The great
mass of Parisians are staunch to the standards set by
France as a whole, but the Paris seen by the visitor is
merely cosmopolitan. Precisely the same criticism may
be levelled at the West End of London but not, I think,
with the same justice. The garish ugliness of Piccadilly
Circus finds its counterpart in Paris, but it is doubtful
whether the countryfolk who visit the West End of

London find even that portion of the city quite so un-representative of national life and manners as French countryfolk find the centre of their capital city. To the resident Londoner, there is, of course, nothing artificial in London; it is just London, and no doubt the same applies to the Parisians' attitude towards Paris, yet the gulf between the French countryside and its capital always seems to me far wider than that between the English country-side and its capital. Possibly this is due to the difference in size between the two countries. To countryfolk born and bred a great city inevitably seems strange, bewildering, and exotic, yet it would be difficult to imagine a greater contrast than that between the midinette of the Paris boulevards and the simple, patient, hard-working, peasant wife of France.

For the first time in my experience there was a dearth of porters at the Gare du Nord, due to the fact that France was steadily mobilising. I do not propose to enlarge upon the excitement of a taxi-drive from that station to the Gare du Lyon, for this is a stock tourist subject. Suffice to say, that in spite of the driving, which appeared to border upon the miraculous, we arrived safely. There are fewer accidents in Paris than in London, and this is probably due to the quick reaction time of the Latin temperament.

While waiting for our train to Grenoble, we dined at a restaurant opposite the station. It is always a source of wonder to the visitor to Paris that so many restaurants can not only exist but apparently thrive. It would be interesting to know how many Parisians eat their meals

nder their own roofs. The Englishman is often accused
f lack of imagination, but to my mind nothing can be
more unimaginative than a Parisian restaurant. I do not
mean in the matter of food, for he would be a brave
man who criticised French gastronomy, but in the surroundings in which food is eaten. No doubt the French
love of food is responsible for the mirrors which surround
he diner. Everywhere he looks he sees, actually or re-
lected, other people eating, and he is able in various
directions to observe himself similarly occupied. French
restaurants exist simply and solely to cater for the science
of eating. In England, however, eating is not so much a
matter of gastronomy as atmosphere. It is of more importance to the Englishman to know that Dr Johnson
once dined in the same establishment than to know that
the beefsteak is succulently cooked and tastefully embel-
ished, and he is only too glad to pay for the privilege.
Artfully shaded lights, old oak beams and tradition mean
far more to him than scientific and imaginative cooking.
He takes what he gets, the rest is atmosphere and tradition.

Such reflections inevitably lead to the conclusion that
the Frenchman is a realist. Realism is fundamental in the
French character. When the Frenchman eats he is concerned only with eating, when he loves he is concerned
only with loving, and when he makes war he is concerned
only with making war. The talk about Latin sentiment is
nonsense; the French are the least sentimental of all races
and the greatest realists. Hence the Maginot Line.

The journey through the night towards Grenoble was
not very comfortable, for we had decided, on grounds of

economy, not to book a sleeping compartment, and in addition to ourselves our compartment contained a young French artillery officer and a sailor, which made it impossible for us to put our feet up. Frenchmen, I have always noticed, slumber peacefully in any position, and appear never to want to put their feet up. Englishmen however, endure agonies if they cannot raise their feet above floor level. Possibly the British climate and a heritage of gout and rheumatism have something to do with this?

Although we travelled on the P.L.M. Railway, which I have been told on good authority stands for Pour la Morgue, the night passed without accident. Truth compels me to admit that I have only been in one French railway accident. This took place near Lyon. I was slumbering peacefully when I awoke to find myself on the floor of the compartment beneath a pile of other passengers and luggage from the racks. Among the passengers was a tall, sad-faced young man, a courier as it transpired, and when we had sorted ourselves out, and tended to our bruises and abrasions, he said quite calmly: "Don't be alarmed, ladies and gentlemen, this is nothing. A little while ago I was travelling in the Riviera when there was a serious collision. I was among the survivors and was being transferred from the scene of the accident in another train when the engine of that blew up." English people are a trifle unfair to the French in the matter of their railways. I have travelled from Marseilles to Paris at night through almost continuous dense fog and have arrived on the stroke of time. What English train could perform this feat? It goes to show that French signalling arrangements are highly efficient, though certain cynical persons have affirmed that I was lucky.

The night was pleasantly cool, and, to our unbounded surprise, the window was not only opened but allowed to remain open. Thus I am debarred from making any of those time-honoured witticisms which have to do with the conflict of opinion between the fresh-air loving Englishman and the fug-loving foreigner as to the ventilation of a railway compartment. Truth further compels me to state that the French sailor left the corridor door wide open, and that I, feeling chilly, stealthily closed it. I feel that I must endeavour to rehabilitate the self-respect of the British nation by quoting a notice which I suspect is entirely fictitious. It runs: "In the event of a dispute between passengers as to whether the window shall be opened or shut, the dispute shall be referred to the conductor and the window then shut."

Dawn found me stretching my legs in the corridor. The train was passing across a well-cultivated plain intersected with the usual rows of poplars, and dotted with crinkly tiled farmsteads and cottages. In the middle distance, a smooth-surfaced river threaded level water-meadows. Here and there lay drifts of thin white mist, and these added to the impression of distance, so that the plain seemed to stretch endlessly eastwards. As I gazed, the glowing disc of the sun rose into a cloudless sky. It leapt up beyond a high irregular edge forming the crest of a great line of hills, spanning the whole width of the eastern horizon. It came to me with a sudden queer thrilling feeling that I was looking at the Alps. I remembered then, as though it were yesterday, how, as a boy, I had gazed thus from the window of a train and first seen the Alps. Age and experience may dim the vision of high mountains, but I never fail to recapture something of that initial exaltation when for the first time in a mountaineering holiday I see the far-off loom of the high mountains.

It is a queer thing this feeling men have for mountains. How is it that some can look unstirred upon a scene that will rouse emotion in others? How is it that some are alive to beauty, and others are not? Is not the Buddhist theory that we go from life to life retaining not memory but instinctive knowledge the most logical explanation? Some have gained knowledge, others have yet to gain it. If this is so, then I am thankful that I have gained this knowledge of beauty, that I can gaze at a high hill and know its beauty, and sense my destiny in the quietness and peace of Nature. If this is spiritual progress then ours is a gracious and glorious journey, and ugliness is but a passing phase to set off beauty and render its value perceptible to the spirit, just as strife and unhappiness are the perfecters of peace and happiness, a paradox which when understood lifts one edge of the veil from the mystery of human existence.

Quickly the sun lifted over the Alps. The mists were infused with opal, the river was transmuted to a stream of gold and distantly the great hills grew and grew in the eastern sky.

An hour or two later we were past Lyon and among

the foothills of the Alps. This is a curiously tip-tilted country of stratified limestone; the earth has been eased up in bits and pieces so that one may walk up a slope of pasture and forest only to be brought up short by a sheer precipice. These first uplifts of the Alps have a charm of their own, and for anyone who wishes to walk and camp, here is a district open in nature, and commanding varied and beautiful views.

Grenoble is one of the finest cities in France. It is built of a light-coloured stone, and is tidy and neat. Its position at the junction of the Isère and Drac valleys makes it an important military centre. It is strongly fortified and any army that managed to force the Alpine passes would be hard put to it to break through to the French lowlands.

As we had several hours to wait for a motor-bus to La Bérarde, we refreshed ourselves first of all with a bath at an hotel. Selling a bath to an Englishman is, on the Continent, still in the nature of a ritualistic procedure. First of all the bath must be ordered and booked at the bureau. The bather is then passed on in turn to the concierge, the lift-man, a "boots", and finally to the corridor woman in whose domain the bathroom is situated. I have had some remarkable baths in my time, but the most remarkable of all was at an inn in the Austrian Tyrol, in 1922. There my demand for a bath produced, first of all, incredulity and amazement, then amusement, and finally a resigned determination, as much as to say, "We have heard, even read, that Englishmen must have baths. Well, here is an Englishman, he wants a bath—he shall have it." An hour or so later, I was conducted

21

down to the cellar. In the floor of this there was a hollow, into which a quantity of hot water had been poured. Undeterred I had my bath, but I had an uneasy feeling at the same time that more than one pair of eyes watched the operation, and I fancied I heard titterings.

In the matter of baths and five-o'clock tea, the Englishman is gradually coming into his own on the Continent, where both of these functions are regarded as lucrative side-lines by hoteliers, who know very well that, although they may charge exorbitantly for a bath, the Englishman must still have it. In this connection, I recollect the tragic story of a Scotsman. With native canniness he compounded for his baths over a lengthy period. Unhappily however, he had to return home after only a few days. The hotel proprietor was ready and willing to meet him over the matter of pension terms, but resolutely declined to refund his bath money.

The ceremony of the bath over, we watched the world go by from an out-of-door café. Grenoble is a famous tourist centre and we saw numerous English people. Amongst them was a fashionably dressed party in an immaculate Rolls-Royce, complete with chauffeur, cigars, and vase of flowers. They alighted, languidly sipped coffee and departed. Then came a group of British cyclists, members of the Cyclists' Touring Club, sunburned and fit. They chaffed the waiter, ordered their drinks in Cockney English, which was immediately understood, and departed amid broad smiles. I dare say they were better ambassadors of Britain than the exquisites in the Rolls-Royce.

After lunch we ascended by *téléférique* to Fort Rabot, which is a thousand feet above the town, and enjoys an extensive panorama of the neighbouring hills and mountains. Mont Blanc, which is visible from this belvedere in clear weather, was concealed by haze, but we saw the outpost peaks of the Dauphiné Alps and noted that the snow-line was unusually low, this being due to storms during the spring and early summer.

Then we boarded the motor-coach, which for the sum of sixty francs conveys the traveller from Grenoble to La Bérarde, a distance of fifty miles. It was an ancient open type of vehicle, and the driver appeared also to be the proprietor of the small café from which it started. We both had a profound respect for the skill of the French driver and this was increased a hundredfold during the journey. In outward appearance there was nothing remarkable about our chauffeur. He was a short, podgy man, attired in nondescript clothing and a faded cloth cap. The stub of a cigarette was parked behind one ear, and he had a lazy confiding smile. But beneath a very ordinary outward appearance lurked a driving skill and nerve which would have turned the countenance of many a driver in the Brooklands Mountain Handicap a pea-green with wondering envy.

On the road to Le Bourg-d'Oisans, there was little opportunity for him to display his skill, except in a solitary encounter with another car which cut in recklessly and maliciously, for this is a wide and well-graded thoroughfare, linking Grenoble with Briançon. Jim and I had previously pictured the Dauphiné Alps as a primitive

23

region of primitive roads, into which only the more enterprising amongst tourists venture. The journey to La Bérarde completely disillusioned us. For one thing, the road as far as Le Bourg-d'Oisans resembled in its traffic density one of the great British arterial roads, for another the Val Romanche is a dull valley at the best of times and acrid smoke from numerous factories pollutes the atmosphere. It was a dismal introduction to the wilder mountain group of the Alps.

Le Bourg-d'Oisans is a popular tourist resort and its narrow streets were crammed with motor-cars of every type, horse-power, and description. We halted there for refreshments, then, continuing on our way, passed from the Val Romanche into the Val Vénéon at the head of which is situated La Bérarde. There is no through route in this valley, and the road is narrow and tortuous. Providence undoubtedly watched over our driver. His usual method when rounding a corner on the narrow road was to go as fast as possible and rely on his horn regardless of the fact that anyone coming in the opposite direction would be sounding *his* horn for all he was worth. It was only by sheer luck that we did not meet another car on a corner. We did, however, encounter a motor-coach shortly after turning a hairpin bend and were only able to pull up with a yard or two to spare, after which it was necessary to back, in order to allow the other coach to pass, to the very edge of a precipitous drop, a performance which evoked our unqualified admiration.

The scenery conformed closely to our expectations

24

he Val Vénéon is typical of the district, a narrow valley
ith precipitous craggy sides rising towards rugged rock
eaks. Stunted pine-trees derive scanty nourishment from
he stony soil, and torrents dash furiously down the steep
illsides. Jim summed it up very aptly when he said, "It
eminds me of a scene from 'Dracula'; only the bats are
hissing."

Grandeur, sublimity, austerity, wildness, these were our
rst impressions of the Dauphiné Alps. It was not until
ter that we began to appreciate the beauty of this
ountry, which is unlike any other Alpine district, not
xcepting some of the sheer-sided valleys of Canton
larus and the Bernese Oberland.

I should not like to live in a Dauphiné valley. I should
eel shut in and depressed. I should want to climb out of
in order to see a little further than the rift of sky vouch-
afed by the towering mountain-sides and rocky defiles.
et people do live in the Val Vénéon, and not only live,
ut enjoy the process, to judge from the smiling faces we
ow and again met with along the road. At various
illages and hamlets we stopped for passengers and
efreshments. I do not know whether it was the refreshments, or the nature of the road, but our driving approxi-
nated more and more closely to the Brooklands tradition,
nd we began heartily to wish ourselves at La Bérarde.

The most dangerous section of the road was inappropri-
tely the last five miles between St. Christophe and La
Bérarde. Here, after a steep climb, which had the
omforting effect of reducing our speed, the road
raversed the mountain-side in a manner analogous with

that of a serpent. We could have borne this had there n
been sheer drops from the edge of it. Our driver took
flat out; he would rush at terrifying speed towards
bend, round would come the wheel, round would go th
heavy coach with shrieking tyres, then, almost before l
had finished twisting the wheel one way, he had to twi
it the other way for the next curve as hard as he coul
and round we would screech, our wheels a few inch
from the edge of the precipice.

I shall never cease to admire my companion's behaviou
during this nerve-racking time. Lifting his eyes from tl
terrifying prospect of immediate and violent death, an
apparently releasing his mind from all trivialities such as
possible error of judgment, a burst tyre, or the failure c
the steering gear, he enquired in measured accents th
names of certain peaks that were visible up the valley.

Then, lo and behold, the last curve and the last precipic
were safely behind! The road lay along the floor of th
valley and ended in a little village of tall, whitewashe
houses, La Bérarde.

Profoundly thankful to Providence we clambered ou
of the motor-coach, and stealing one last look of awe a
our driver, who had removed the cigarette stub fron
behind his ear and was puffing at it with an expression o
bored detachment, made haste to seek for accommo
dation. We had anticipated no difficulty in this respec
when we left England, but we had already learned tha
Dauphiné is one of the most popular holiday districts in
France, and a glance at the parked masses of cars wa
sufficient to assure us that beds were doubtful in the

xtreme. So it proved. We made for the principal hotel,
aly to be told in that lofty manner which characterises
e hotel proprietor who is complacently aware that all
s rooms are full up with guests that there was not a
ed to be had. It was my badge of honorary membership
f the French Alpine Club that saved us. The manager's
yes strayed to it and he was visibly affected.

"Yes, messieurs, I think it may be possible to give you
room, that is, if you do not mind sharing one, and have
o objection to the annexe."

We assured him we had no objection to the annexe and
ere forthwith escorted thither. It is often the moun-
ineer's lot to sleep in an annexe, for when he moves
out he is not able to book accommodation in advance.
a this respect, he who plants himself at one centre scores
eavily.

It would appear that the principal object of an hotel
roprietor who builds an annexe is not merely to cater
or an overflow of guests, but to impress upon his guests
y contrast how desirable are the amenities of the hotel.
o it was in this case, and I will content myself by remark-
ug that the annexe in which we found ourselves was that
ind of annexe where you dare not look under the bed.
One word alone of A. D. Godley's verse need be changed:

> They will dine on mule and marmot
> And on mutton made of goats
> They will face the various horrors
> Of Dauphiné table d'hôtes.

Two other British mountaineers, Messrs D. Cox and
eter Lloyd, were present and to them we recounted our

impressions of the motor journey. They replied that when they had travelled along the road, the motor-coach had narrowly escaped being struck by falling stones. Mountaineering is certainly not the most dangerous of Alpine pastimes.

The surroundings of La Bérarde bear out the reputation of Dauphiné for stoniness. There are a few pastures wrested from the stones by the industrious peasants, but these only serve to emphasise the harsher features, the tumbled boulders, scree slopes, crags, and precipices. Our first impression of the Val Vénéon was of a valley similar to that in which Sinbad found his diamonds; a closer look, however, revealed that Nature had done her best to beautify the barrenness. She had sown innumerable flowers, and so well had she succeeded in this pleasant task that my later impressions of Dauphiné came to be not stones but flowers.

We dined in a fly-blown, low-ceilinged room in which were some two dozen guests. On the walls were various advertisements and some cheap German lithographs of pre-war vintage, one depicting wasp-waisted ladies and bearded gentlemen admiring a vista of Mont Blanc, not an inspiring picture and one which became depressing when gazed at too long.

Why is a French roll delicious and French bread abominable? This does not apply to all French bread but it does to the bread of Dauphiné, and, unhappily, rolls and coffee of a quality that makes breakfast a meritorious function in many parts of France are lacking in the smaller Alpine resorts, where even the butter has flavour of goat about it, and the honey is no less nthetic than it is in Switzerland. Primitivism may or ay not be desirable, but primitivism which apes civilisa- on is undesirable. The early mountaineers in the Alps ere undoubtedly flea-bitten, but at least they had the tisfaction that the primitive brings to civilised man. he modern Alpine mountaineer has often neither the ne nor the other, and has to go far afield to discover the ys of simple living, unless he is sufficiently enterprising render himself independent of inns and hotels by mping.

After dinner we refreshed ourselves with a stroll. The eather during the past few days had been fine in auphiné. It was still fine, although we did not entirely pprove of a smooth-looking cloud in the north. The oon was rising; its rays had not yet penetrated into the alley, but they lit the great crags opposite, which hung the stars like a spectral curtain.

When travelling it is impossible to be peaceful, for pid motion, whether on land or through the air, is imical of true peace. Haste is synonymous with worry nd impatience, and these, in their turn, are scarcely com- atible with the greater human qualities of patience, oughtfulness and consideration for others. It is pleasant arrive in the mountains after a rapid journey by rail nd road. For a day or more the traveller has seen the ountryside flash past him as a welter of fleeting and lusive impressions. There is something unreal about apid transit from one place to another, except in the ltimate change of scene. He who girdles the world in a

29

fast-moving aeroplane sees less than he who sits himse
down in a quiet country place.

Jim and I had come to a halt among the mountain.
They were around us, unmoving, looming against th
stars. We could hear them, a soothing note of runnin
water, constant and enduring; we could feel them, no
only beneath our feet, not only their cold breath, but a
a presence, not the mere presence of so many tons of roc
and snow, but a spiritual balm, the blessing and bene
diction of changeless things.

CHAPTER II

LES BANS

E awoke next morning to hear a peal of thunder and
patter of hail. Our suspicions of the previous evening
d not proved unfounded. Slate-coloured clouds were
ing up from the west and crackling concussions of
under reverberated amongst the peaks.

In the matter of Alpine weather, I consider myself a
nah and I remarked as much to Jim, with a sort of
oomy satisfaction. His reply was: "Well, I'm usually
cky, so perhaps we shall cancel each other out." I could
ly hope that what he said was true, for I had come to
ok upon my ill-luck with Alpine weather as proverbial
d inevitable. What usually happens is that I arrive in
e Alps at a time when everyone is complaining of the
ought. On the evening of my arrival, dark clouds
ther and on all sides I hear people say, "At last we shall
ve some rain." It is true, there is rain, and snow, and
ery kind of climatic unpleasantness, continuing without
termission for the next two or three weeks. In disgust
eturn to England, with the idea of finishing my holiday
North Wales or the Lake District. I arrive back to find
at there has been a drought ever since I left. Headlines
corate the newspapers—farmers, it is said, are frantic,
d prayers for rain are being said in the churches. A day

31

or so later I arrive at Seathwaite or some such normall
wet place in the hills, to find every marsh and stream drie
up. It has not rained for over two months the inhabitan'
tell me with a gloomy despair. "Don't worry, it will no'
I've come," I answer. They look at me unbelieving an
incredulous, but sure enough that self-same night rai
begins to fall and continues to fall without intermissio
for the remainder of my holiday. Soon after returnin
home I receive post cards from friends still in the Alp
the Lake District, or North Wales. "Why on earth di
you go back to England?" enquire the former. "Tl
weather has been marvellous since you left."—"What
pity your holiday came to an end!" write the latter. "W
are having perfect weather."

It was, therefore, with feelings of surprise and amaz
ment that I noticed a distinct improvement in the weathe
towards midday. The thunder-clouds receded with baffle
growls, the sun broke through, and a rainbow arche
itself prettily across the valley. Was it possible that n
Jonah had met its match in Jim? At all events it ha
received a temporary set-back, and I agreed enthusiast
cally with Jim's suggestion that we should set off in
mediately towards the Pilatte hut with the idea
climbing Les Bans, a peak of 12,040 feet, on the morro
I even went so far as to suggest in my turn that, inste:
of spending the night in the crowded hut, we should sle
in the open, taking with us our bivouac tent and sleepin;
bags for the purpose, a proposal to which he acquiesce
with enthusiasm.

The weather had almost completely cleared whe

hortly after lunch, we set out from La Bérarde, and only
n occasional drift of warm rain added its pearls to the
erbage as we trudged up the valley.

Now that our mountaineering holiday had properly
egun, my first reaction was not, I fear, that of *joie de
ivre* and unbounding energy; but a loathing for my
ucksack which seemed unconscionably heavy; further-
nore, as I laboured up the path, I seemed to melt all over
ke an ice-cream on a summer's day. In three words, I
vas out of training. Let me express at once my un-
ounded admiration for those persons who are always in
raining, who skip, run, and jump before breakfast, who
lunge themselves in ice-cold water, who cut out this and
hat in the matter of food and drink, who stride over
niles and miles and miles of the countryside every week-
nd, passing every public-house with an air of insufferable
elf-denial and virtue, who twist and writhe their stomach
nuscles and add knobbly inches to their biceps. I do none
f these things, I am much too lazy; therefore, for the first
ay or two of an Alpine holiday, I am out of training, and
peak of 12,000 feet and a walk of not more than twelve
ours is as much as I can comfortably manage. Jim, being
1 the army, and incidentally twelve years younger than
ne, was, of course, in training. He had suggested Les
3ans as our first expedition, and had obtained details from
climbing friend, who described the ascent as an excellent
ttle training climb. All the same, Les Bans is 12,040 feet
igh and is described by Baedeker as "very difficult; descent
early as long", and I began to wonder what schemes
vere afoot for the mortification of my untrained flesh.

The worst of being out of training is that there is a lack of co-ordination between mind and muscle. The untrained one proceeds uphill in fits and starts, not with that slow, deliberate, rhythmical output of energy and movement which is the sure sign of good training. The feet are not put down exactly where it is intended they should be, and a really stony slog is productive of many unshed tears. So it was on this occasion; the path seemed exceptionally stony and rough; my rucksack grew steadily heavier, and through eyes smarting with salty sweat, I watched Jim enviously as he strode uphill with never a drop of moisture on his brow, serenely unconscious of his labouring companion.

An hour later the path debouched on to the Alp de Carrelet. The weather had almost completely cleared now, and only the thinnest of thin blue showers was being wafted by the warm west wind across the precipice of the Ailefroide. Is there a nobler view in Dauphiné than that from the Alp de Carrelet? Imagine a meadow of brilliant green, all the more brilliant by contrast with the savage surrounding precipices, dotted with small feather-like pines, which unite to sweep up a hillside in a full-fledged forest. Beyond this gentle foreground is a background of precipice, a huge, rust-coloured curtain 6,000 feet in height, mellow and remote in the afternoon sun, crested by a thin ribbon of silvery, wind-turned snow.

On the Alp de Carrelet there is a hut at which climbers spend the night before undertaking one of the numerous expeditions in the locality. Experience of the Alps has taught us to associate good viewpoints with refreshments

and a few minutes later we were seated in the hut,
a rough stone dwelling resembling a hop-picker's hut,
drinking light French beer at the moderate sum of
three francs a bottle. A number of tourists were doing
much the same thing. Most were possessors of ice axes.
The ice axe has taken the place of the walking-stick and
alpenstock with the modern tourist. It is true that it is
neither so useful as a walking-stick, nor so impressive as
an alpenstock with a spiral of place-names and heights
engraved on it, but it confers on its owner a certain
distinction and separates him from that other kind of
tourist who does little walking, and thus does not need
even an ice axe. From an ice axe to a pair of crampons
(climbing-irons) is another step, and though the latter
may never be used, except perhaps as a substitute for
nocks over the boots on the slippery ice of a glacier, their
ferocious appearance is worth something to their intrepid
owner, and they are distinctly useful when placed points
outwards on the back of a rucksack in a customs or
passport queue. A length of rope completes the equipment. I wish I knew how to coil a rope as neatly and as
beautifully as the tourist does. I wish, too, that I could
get the same thrill out of mere possession and exhibition,
but ever since a rude fellow called out to me on the first
occasion that I carried a rope, "Goin' to 'ang yourself,
guv'nor?" I have sedulously sought to conceal this dam-
ing evidence of mental instability. Far be it from me to
gibe at these proud possessors of ice axes, crampons, and
ropes, even though they do no more than walk up to a
hut, spend the following day admiring the view, and

35

walk down again, for I know full well that I, too, went through the stage of owning but not using the tools of mountaineering.

We continued on our way greatly refreshed. After proceeding for a short distance, we came to a point where the path divided. Both branches appeared to continue up the valley, so we took the right-hand one which contours along the mountain-side to the west of the stream. I am glad we did so because we entered upon some of the most flowerful slopes I have ever seen in the Alps, indeed I do not recollect seeing elsewhere in that range so varied and concentrated a number of rare and lovely species.

It was now late in the afternoon and the shadows were gathering in the valley. There was no further doubt as to the weather's immediate intentions; the storm-clouds had all dissolved and we were assured of a fine day for our climb.

Presently we reached the limit of burnable vegetation and cast around for a bivouac site. After scrambling for some time over the steep hillside we found an overhanging boulder, the size of a cottage, which formed a shallow cave, twenty yards from a tumbling stream arched over with an immense drift of avalanche snow. I could see that Jim's professional zeal was aroused by sundry inequalities in the ground, so leaving him to engineer a comfortable platform, I went in search of fuel.

It was the first time I had ever bivouacked at a moderate altitude in the Alps, and I was reminded of camping in similar situations in the Himalayas. I returned with an armful of juniper to find that my companion had excavated and levelled a sleeping-place. Water was not so easy to get. We had to crawl under the vaulted avalanche snow in order to reach the stream, an uncomfortable process as the packed snow above weighed many tons.

At length all was ready for a meal. Before leaving England, we had weighed the pros and cons of a pocket "Primus", but had decided against it on the score of weight. Instead, we had provided ourselves with a methylated cooker of a type which has a burner consisting of a number of holes round a central orifice into which the methylated is poured. The scheme is that having three-quarters filled the orifice, the methylated is lit; this heats the burner until presently the spirit vaporises and jets of flame emerge from the holes. It is a simple contrivance and reasonably efficient, except in a wind; then it is the very devil. On this occasion there was no wind, and we vowed that the tea we brewed was perfect.

There is no doubt that mountaineering, or for that matter any hard exercise, in the open air makes a man appreciate his food and drink, and the most ordinary tea acquires a bouquet and fragrance undreamt of in civilisation.

Tea was followed by soup. In the matter of soup, I am not only knowledgeable, I am expert. Once, when staying at a hut, I made a soup that contained sixteen ingredients. My climbing companion who partook of it said that it was unique, but a little later, after looking at me for some time without saying a word, tersely remarked that it was

a beautiful night outside and went out to look at it. I
was only too glad to follow him.

On this occasion I was circumscribed in the matter of
ingredients, and the soup consisted merely of a packet or
two of "Maggi" powders. But for all that it proved
excellent, and we vowed that our bivouac was superior in
comfort to any hut.

Our supper eaten, we lit our juniper fire, and lolling
back in our cave smoked our pipes. The evening was
supremely calm. On high, the crest of the Ailefroide was
pink, against a sky of deepening blue, and at the head of
the valley beyond the serene curve of the Pilatte glacier
stood Les Bans, a graceful mountain built up of sweeping
ridges, aglow in the declining sun. As we watched, peace-
ably puffing at our pipes, the golden tide ebbed heaven-
wards. As the dusk gathered the light breezes died away
and the smoke of our fire stood up with scarcely a quiver.
There was no sound save for the constant percussion of
the glacier torrent. It seemed scarcely credible that little
more than forty-eight hours ago we were in the
maelstrom of London. In retrospect civilisation seemed
strangely futile and purposeless. I remembered the remark
of a Himalayan native. He said: "We have heard of your
wonderful machines that go very quickly through the air
and across the earth. But tell me, does it make a man
happier to go from one place to another quicker than we
go on a pony?"

The mental reactions consequent upon spending one
day in London and the next day in the High Alps are
curious. It would be difficult, to begin with, to imagine

a more abrupt change of scene. Then it is undoubtedly true that during the first few days of his holiday, the mountaineer tends to be obsessed by the time factor, the predominant factor of civilised life. A great many mountaineers never escape from time, and that this is so is proved by a slavish adhesion to it when making or subsequently recording a climb. A glance at any climbing publication will prove the truth of this assertion. There is, of course, a certain technical interest about "times" in mountaineering. Furthermore, some attention to time is necessary for reasons of convenience and, on occasion, safety, but I have never been able to understand the type of mind that cannot escape from time on a mountain, and that must needs climb pocket-book and pencil in hand noting the time at which such and such an object is reached. For me, perhaps the greatest enjoyment in mountaineering lies in escaping from my normal enslavement to time. The fact that I may have crossed the bergschrund at 3.15 a.m., reached the ridge at 6.25, traversed the first gendarme at 7.10, and gained the summit at 9.42 is of little or no interest, nor does it interest me to know the time of someone else on the same route. I suspect that this abhorrence of watch-in-hand climbing is due to the fact that I enjoy the scenery of mountains as much as I like climbing mountains. I am, however, bound to admit that were the world made up of people like myself, it would be an impracticable sort of affair, and from a material standpoint decidedly primitive. It would rub along in a happy-go-lucky *mañana* manner; but it would at least be contented, happy, and without wars, for no one can fight a war nowadays who is not a slave to time.

In the present instance time as an associate and reflection of human activity no longer mattered. It was measured only by the deepening dusk and the kindling stars. There was no time in the constant note of the glacier torrent, nor was time measured by a multitude of trivial thoughts. We were content to meditate, to allow ourselves to assimilate without effort, the beauty and peace of eventide.

Meanwhile our fire flamed and crackled merrily, and as daylight waned lit up our cave with its ruddy glow. The fragrant smell of the burning juniper transported us back to the early days of Alpine climbing, the days of Edward Whymper, Leslie Stephen, John Ball, and A. W. Moore. Perhaps the pioneers shared our camp-fire. It needed little imagination to picture ourselves bivouacking, not for a popular expedition, but an unclimbed peak, thrilled with the subtle joy that comes to a man on the eve of new adventure into the unknown, the prospect of setting foot where no human foot has trodden before.

The fire died down and the moon rose. The crags high above us shone against the stars, then slowly the pale radiance crept valleywards. It brought with it a chilling feeling, a promise of frost, and we made haste to get into our sleeping-bags while still warm. There was no occasion to employ the tent, which was intended only for an emergency, and we used it as a coverlet.

Jim had engineered a wide platform, and we lay side

by side in perfect comfort. Presently I heard him breathing deeply and regularly and knew he slept, but it was a
long time before I followed suit. I did not even want to
sleep; I was content to gaze upwards at the stars, and
the brilliant orb of the moon sailing its precise course
through the heavens. Gradually, with increasing sleep-
iness, there came to me a feeling of unreality as I contemplated the mysteries of space; the mountains seemed
to shrink and recede and the roll of the glacier torrent
was resolved into celestial music . . .

We both awoke later, in my case a trifle chilly as I
had the outside berth, and the earth beneath me was
damp. It was midnight or thereabouts, and much of
the romance had vanished from the proceedings. Jim
presently went off to sleep again, but I lay awake for
the remainder of the night. I have had many sleepless
nights in the mountains, particularly on Mount Everest,
and very long some of them seemed. The present night
was no exception and, as I lay awake with a cold spine
and stiff shoulder-blades, the world no longer appeared so
beautiful as it had done when my stomach was warm
and well filled. There is a sordid fact connected with all
human activity; it is that aesthetic enjoyment is dependent
on a warm and well-nourished body, and that failing this
condition the loveliest mountain views may be contemplated with a cold loathing. This was a case in point; I
longed for dawn and activity, and thought wistfully
of those civilised comforts which I had affected to
despise.

Dawn came at last, the faintest paling of the sky behind

the moon-bathed cliffs of the Ailefroide. In happier circumstances I should not have noticed it, but now I
roused my blissfully slumbering companion.

"It's getting light," I told him.

He received this intelligence with an incredulous grunt,
gave a snort and a heave and settled down once more to
slumber.

But I had had enough of bivouacking and went off to
get water. After a tricky scramble in the dark under the
snow arch I filled the saucepan, only to slip on the way
back and upset it. By the time it had been refilled the
remarks I had to make about breakfasting in the dark,
with particular reference to saucepans, had effectively
roused Jim into a show of activity.

Hot tea was good; it was more than good, indeed
beyond the range of laudatory adjectives. It put life into
our cold stiffened limbs and rekindled the damped fires of
optimism and enthusiasm.

By the time we had finished our breakfast it was light
enough to see, so packing our rucksacks we set off for
Les Bans, having cached our bivouac equipment under a
boulder.

The moon showed shrunken and pale as we trudged up
the stony path towards the Pilatte hut, and ahead the
crest of our peak shone with the first cold pallor of day.
We both felt in that stupid, drowsy state peculiar to the
early hours of the morning, when vitality is at its lowest.
Many writers have enlarged on the excitement of an
early start in the Alps, I have been guilty of this myself,
but years of indiscretion, if I may put it thus, now

compel me to state emphatically that not only is there nothing exciting or romantic about it, but that it is a thoroughly disagreeable proceeding which I associate with a stomach that complains bitterly for not being allowed to complete its normal digestive processes in peace, and a certain mental state best described as fed-upness with everyone and everything.

However, it will be inferred that if mountaineering happiness is primarily a matter of efficient circulation and unimpaired digestion, then there is nothing like a good brisk walk for setting things right. So it proved in the present instance; an unqualified gastronomical gloom presently disappeared, and was superseded by intelligent interest and even mild enthusiasm.

An hour after leaving our bivouac we came to the Pilatte hut. Outside it was stationed a solitary tourist of doleful demeanour who growled a surly "bon jour, messieurs", which greeting we returned with, what to him must have seemed, a hateful heartiness.

Purely as a matter of interest and inquisitiveness we opened the door of the hut and glanced inside. At least Jim did while I peered over his shoulder. Next instant he staggered back, pulling to the door as he did so. I have never been in a submarine unable to rise from the bed of the sea with the air becoming fouler every minute, but I should imagine that the experience would closely resemble a night spent in the Pilatte hut during the holiday season. Our feelings were summed up by Jim, who turned to me and said in a voice vibrant with emotion, "Thank God we bivouacked, Frank."

43

A few minutes later we trod the frozen surface of the Pilatte glacier. We were still in cold shadow, but we could see the sun shining on the upper *sérac* of the glacier which were silhouetted against the blue sky in all manner of strange poses. We could also see another party evidently bound, like us, for Les Bans.

Tramping uphill over board-hard snow through motionless frosty air was a pleasant preliminary to the more serious work of the day. The glacier was larger and more complicated than we had suspected, but tracks of previous parties obviated the need for route finding, and we mounted in that preoccupied yet negative frame of mind which I always associate with long and un-interesting ascents on easy snow.

Higher up, the glacier was considerably broken and the ice scenery varied and beautiful, broken walls of gleaming ice alternating with widely rifted crevasses. We had to zigzag through the latter, crossing numerous well-frozen snow bridges, and pass beneath a tottery wall of ice some eighty feet in height which appeared ready to crumple up and fall at any moment.

Presently we came out of shadow into brilliant sun-light and plumped ourselves down in the snow for another meal; it was several hours since we had left our bivouac and the inner man had long since passed from active resentment into a dull despair and from dull despair into renewed resentment.

Second breakfast, as all mountaineers know, is a solemn and time-hallowed rite. It marks a transition stage in the day's work, a ceremony differentiating the cold hours of dawn from the exciting prospects of a day's mountaineering.

I forget what we ate, but I believe sardines, raisins, and chocolate were on the menu; and I can never eat the first named without thinking of a friend of mine whose favourite mountaineering diet is sardines and honey, spread together on bread and butter.

Our halt span out into a full half-hour. As we sunned ourselves we noticed with an interest that verged upon incredulity living creatures emerging from the Pilatte hut some 2,000 feet or more beneath us, and remarked that the peaks of Dauphiné, with the exception of the glacier-clad mountains we were climbing, were fully as stony and precipitous as we had anticipated.

Continuing on our way, we made some more zigzags through the intricacies of the glacier, and arrived an hour later at the foot of an ice slope which ended in the east ridge of Les Bans. At its foot this slope was rifted by a formidable bergschrund separating it from the Pilatte glacier on which we stood. The rift was bridged by a tongue of snow at one place, but its upper lip was some fifteen feet high and vertical if not overhanging. The party ahead of us had crossed the snow bridge, scaled the lip, and cut steps up the ice slope. There seemed, therefore, every reason for us to do likewise and profit by the steps they had cut. But to my shame I must record that not only did we not do this, but that we avoided their route altogether and climbed up by an easier way. I, not Jim, was responsible for this decision. I crossed the snow bridge and tried to climb the ice lip, and because it was

45

steep and strenuous work, and because I was hopelessly out of training, I returned to Jim and declared myself in favour of an easier route if such existed. I have not the slightest doubt that Jim could have romped up the ice lip, but he unselfishly agreed with me that we could get up more easily on the left. Our "slink round", as I termed it later, meant traversing horizontally until we were almost beneath the Col de Pilatte, crossing the bergschrund at an easier place, climbing some rocks and snow to the col, and doubling back along the ridge from the latter to the final rocks of Les Bans. In the course of this entirely unnecessary manoeuvre we at least had the satisfaction of treading classic ground, for the bergschrund we crossed was that associated with a dramatic episode during the first passage of the Col de Pilatte by Edward Whymper's party in 1864. The bergschrund was more formidable then and the party, who had crossed the pass in the reverse direction, had to jump down fifteen or sixteen feet, and forward at the same time some seven or eight feet, alighting on a narrow ridge of ice. The first three made the leap successfully. Then came the turn of Whymper's friend Jean Reynaud. The episode is best described in Whymper's own words:

"He came to the edge and made declarations. I do not believe that he was a whit more reluctant to pass the place than we others, but he was infinitely more demonstrative—in a word, he was French. He wrung his hands. 'Oh, what a *diable* of a place!' 'It is nothing, Reynaud,' I said, 'it is nothing.' 'Jump,' cried the others, 'jump.' But he turned round, as far as one can do such a thing in

46

an ice-step, and covered his face with his hands, ejaculating, 'Upon my word, it is not possible. No! No!! No!!! it is not possible.'

"How he came over I scarcely know. We saw a toe—it seemed to belong to Moore; we saw Reynaud a flying body, coming down as if taking a header into water—with arms and legs all abroad, his leg of mutton flying in the air, his baton escaped from his grasp; and then we heard a thud as if a bundle of carpets had been pitched out of a window."

No such excitement befell us, and a little later we found ourselves on the sharp snow crest separating the Col de Pilatte from the rocks of Les Bans. The party ahead of us had climbed the mountain and were descending, and we paused to watch them. There were three of them, one, the middlemost man on the rope, being both bulky and clumsy, so much so that we watched almost anxiously. Largely because of him, the party was moving slowly, and the loose rocks they knocked down more than deterred us from attempting the climb until they were safely off the mountain. Seen *en face* the rocks appeared wellnigh vertical, but the lie to their steepness and difficulty was given by the climbing method employed by the party we were watching, particularly that of the fat man, a method destructive to the seat of the trousers. It was not an inspiring spectacle and it became positively alarming when the fat man's feet shot from under him on a patch of ice and he subsided with a jolt on some rocks. However, as I told myself, who were we to criticise? I, at least, should put up an equally undignified performance on this, my first expedition of the season.

They were down at last, and after exchanging greetings, and seeing that they were out of range of any stones *we* might knock down, we moved along the ridge to the rocks and began to ascend.

The climb proved an excellent first expedition of the season, and the rocks, though steep in places, were neither too difficult nor too sensational, and were excellent in promoting that harmony of mind and muscle which is the hallmark of skill and practice in mountaineering.

Unhappily, the pleasure of the ascent was marred by severe altitude headaches. I have suffered from these headaches before, both in the Alps and Himalayas, and they always result from a climb to an elevation in excess of 10,000 feet the first day. I do not know if they are peculiar to mountaineers because, while many members of Everest expeditions have been prostrated by them on arrival at Thangu bungalow in Sikkim, which is situated at a height of only 11,000 feet, tourists frequently visit the bungalow without similar ill effects. If there is a worse form of headache I do not know it. It begins at the base of the skull and drives knives of pain through the head to the eyes. Every movement, every jar of the foot on the ground, is agony, and when vomiting supervenes it does little or nothing to alleviate the pain. My only consolation was that Jim complained of a similar headache. This sounds a selfish statement, but there are few human beings, however Christian or humane, who do not derive

48

THE BERGSCHRUND BELOW LES BANS

a vicarious satisfaction from knowing that their ills are shared by a companion. Therefore while I said "Bad luck" to Jim, when he complained of *his* headache, I was secretly glad that I was not the only one to suffer.

Had it not been for our headaches, we should have enjoyed better than we did the scramble to the summit. Fortunately memory has the inestimable advantage of eliminating physical sensation and promoting to the fore, often in false perspective, latent mental and spiritual enjoyment. Thus I remember the climb as interesting, the weather as perfect, and the views as extensive and beautiful. Memory tells me that the rocks were pleasant to handle, that they were soaked with sun, and seemed almost to breathe warmth as we climbed up them. What memory does not tell me is that at the time I had a bursting head, and that I swore to myself over and over again that come what might never would I climb a peak as high as Les Bans the first day of a mountaineering holiday.

Moving for the most part both together we progressed rapidly, at least Jim did, while I laboured in the rear, a prey to my lack of training which transformed an easy and pleasant rock climb into a sweating, puffing, unharmonious labour.

My head was feeling like a Mills bomb which has just had its trigger released when, of a sudden, rocks no longer loomed above, and we trod with dramatic unexpectedness the level summit of Les Bans.

Headachy and sick we sank down on sun-warmed slabs of schistose. "That's that," said Jim, with the air of

49

one to whom the climb has seemed unexpectedly and disappointingly short. "Thank heavens!" I replied fervently.

A few minutes' rest improved our malaise and we were able to take stock of the view. The Dauphiné Alps certainly confirmed our first impressions of wildness and grandeur. What we saw was not fantastic and bizarre like the Dolomites, nor serene and well ordered like the principal ranges of the Alps, but something in between. There were glaciers to be seen, in particular the Pilatte glacier which curved away at our feet, but these were incidental to the main theme, which was an intricate jumble of savage rock peaks, not peaks with sweeping ridges and faces like those on the main watershed of the Alps, but mountains whose principal characteristics are steepness and complexity. To an orthodox mountaineer the view from Les Bans is depressing rather than elevating. It is uneasy, and somehow incomplete. It is neutral in colour; there are no green alps and smiling pasturelands such as the mountaineer gazes upon from the heights of the Oberland or Mont Blanc; there are no gentle and gracious forms, no shining snowfields and remote wind-fashioned snow edges. Order and methodicity is lacking and, instead, there is a vast untidy mess of rocky mountains and narrow tortuous valleys. The Dauphiné massif is a by-product, a collection of shattered peaks arranged anyhow, not in supreme disregard for ordinary laws like the Dolomites, but rather as an untidy afterthought to the Alps. It is as though Nature had said, "Well, there are the Alps, they look all right, but there's a vacant space here, and I've a lot of stuff left

over, not much snow and ice but any amount of rock;
I'll plank it down here and make the best job I can
with it."

But already I can sense my mountaineering friends
writhing inwardly. To say such things about Dauphiné!
Look at the Meije, the Ecrins, they say; graceful mountains, splendid climbs; this fellow, confound him, is only
writing to annoy—deliberate contentiousness! Therefore,
let me hasten to add that the Dauphiné Alps grow on the
mountaineer. I have recorded here faithfully my first
reactions to these mountains, but later, only a little later,
I came to like Dauphiné better. A conventional mountaineer requires some time to accustom himself to the
unconventional, and unconventional from an architectural standpoint Dauphiné certainly is. During my few
days in this country I came to learn the charm of its
stony valleys, where little flowers peep out in unexpected
places, and the untamed splendour of its peaks and precipices. I learned that it is a range of unsuspected views
and odd and delightful corners, as many of both in a
mile as in any other mountain country I know. Then
there is the spell of the unknown. In point of fact there
is nothing unknown about the peaks of Dauphiné, though
there are many new routes to be made up them, but the
early reputation of inaccessibility gained by this labyrinth
of ridges, gorges, and valleys has never been quite dis-
pelled. It is accurately and meticulously mapped, but the
mountaineer feels that to him personally it is *terra incognita*,
and that he must explore it: in the course of his explora-
tions he will experience much the same feelings that the

pioneers experienced who first worked their way from valley to valley over the intricate ridges. Such then is the charm of this strange country, and if the charm is at first not apparent it becomes perceptible with increasing knowledge and experience.

Apart from general impressions, what did we see from the summit of Les Bans? First and foremost our gaze sought out the Meije, 13,065 feet which, except in the matter of height—Les Ecrins, 13,450, is the highest summit in Dauphiné—is the undisputed monarch of the district. It also enjoys the distinction of being the last great Alpine peak to have been climbed, and this not so much on account of its forbidding appearance as the sheer difficulty of the climbing. The Meije is unmistakable from any direction, a square-built mass with a long summit ridge bristling with towers, with one conical-shaped point, the Grand Pic, at the westernmost end, to complete the resemblance to a Norman fortress. Les Ecrins was not seen to advantage because of the interposing mass of the Ailefroide. Les Rouies, 11,775 feet, and the Pic d'Olan, 11,740, are the highest peaks to the west, the latter a beautiful wall-sided mountain renowned among rock climbers.

Yet we were little concerned with topographical details. For one thing we were too headachy and tired; for another the sun blazed down with lambent intensity, and there was not a breath of wind to temper its heat. It is not often that the mountaineer finds himself frizzling on an Alpine summit 12,000 feet high, and Jim, feeling that he had done all that was required of him in the matter of the view and topographical identification, settled himself back to a boulder with his handkerchief over his face and fell fast asleep. I would have followed his example had it not occurred to me that if I did so we might both of us continue to sleep for hours and be benighted in consequence. Therefore I contented myself with a doze.

In this way over an hour passed. It is a curious experience dozing or sleeping on a mountain-top. The mountaineer, half drugged by the sunlight, rouses himself by slow degrees. He sees before him peak, range, and valley shining and unsubstantial like a vision, so much so that it is difficult to separate reality from unreality, and it requires a conscious mental effort to face up to the hard fact that a long, toilsome and difficult descent has to be negotiated. Sleeping on a mountain-top is not always a safe luxury, and I can recollect more than one occasion when I have set off down a difficult climb, yawning and drowsy and an incomplete master of myself for the first minute or two. It is in such moments of physical and mental inertia that accidents may occur.

The descent proved easy, and we rattled down the rocks. Our headaches were finally dissipated by the loss of height, and we both felt in good fettle by the time the ridge was regained. There we decided to descend the ice slope we had avoided on the way up. It was easier than expected, though the vertical lip of the bergschrund needed delicate balance. Jim went first, and after asking for plenty of slack rope, jumped the last ten feet or so down and across the rift, alighting gracefully on a snow ridge forming the lower lip, whence he skidded off down the slope below for a yard or two before coming to a halt in the soft snow of the glacier. I followed, and if my performance was not so dramatic as that of Reynaud's seventy-five years before me, I felt equally ridiculous as I sailed through the air, to alight with an undignified thump, and shoot down pell-mell to my laughing companion.

Thenceforwards we ploughed and glissaded rapidly down the sun-softened snow of the Pilatte glacier. The *séracs* and the crevasses were behind, or so we thought, and we were on smooth unbroken snow when of a sudden down went my feet into a concealed crevasse. It was not a wide crevasse, but wide enough for a lissom mountaineer, and I had a momentary vision of sombre bottle-green depths before I struggled out. The rope was by no means taut, and Jim told me afterwards that he was over the same trap. It was a lesson to us both; nothing could have seemed more innocent than the snow slopes we were on when the incident occurred, and we apostrophised ourselves as fools.

The shadows were lengthening as we passed the Pilatte hut, and scampered down slopes of scree and snow to our bivouac place. We retrieved our equipment and strolled down the flowerful slopes to the Alp de Carrelet, where we quenched our thirst with beer.

Forgotten were our headaches and fatigue as we lolled contentedly outside the Carrelet hut in the late afternoon sun. Life was very good; the clock had moved on a few hours; another mountain memory had been gained. In any dark or evil hours that might lie ahead we could return in spirit to a star-filled night by a juniper fire, sun-warmed rocks and the meadows of the Alp de Carrelet. Such memories endure.

So we lingered a while on the Alp de Carrelet. The sun slipped lower and lower in a cloudless sky, and cool shadows gathered in the valley. Peak and precipice stood immobile in a silent air. Only the stream continued its litany and birds twittered in the hushed pine forest. At such moments earthy man is aware of something greater than his earthiness.

Dusk was falling as we walked down the path to La Bérarde.

CHAPTER III

LES ECRINS

OUR luck with the weather was in the ascendant, and immediately after our return to La Bérarde from Les Bans we determined to climb Les Ecrins, the highest peak in Dauphiné; after this ascent we should be in sufficiently good training to traverse the Meije.

Since Edward Whymper's party made their classic first ascent and traverse in 1864 a number of routes have been made up the mountain. The most popular of these is that by the south rock face from the Col des Avalanches, the descent to La Bérarde being made via the north-west ridge, the Col des Ecrins and the Glacier de la Bonne Pierre. This expedition is usually made from the Temple-Ecrins hut above the Alp de Carrelet, but enquiry elicited the information that the hut had been destroyed by an avalanche, and that another hut was being constructed but was as yet uninhabitable. We determined, therefore, to bivouac in the neighbourhood of the hut.

With only a short walk in prospect it was unnecessary to leave La Bérarde until after lunch, and we spent the morning following upon our ascent of Les Bans idling about the village.

Not so very many years ago La Bérarde was uncon-nected with the outside world by a motor road and delightfully primitive. The Swiss very wisely have deliberately sought to exclude motor-cars from some of their valleys, and one of the charms of Zermatt is that it is possible to walk in the street without being threatened by motorists who nowadays appear to imagine, and not without reason in view of the timorous behaviour of pedestrians, that a road confers on them a divine right of progress. The French, however, possibly for military reasons, have of recent years constructed motor roads in many valleys hitherto only accessible by mule track. It may seem bigoted and die-hard conservatism to denounce motor-cars out of hand, but the sad fact remains that of all man's inventions the internal-combustion engine has been put to the lowest uses. Furthermore, it is smelly and noisy, and the particular brand of tourist it conveys to the Alps often reflects its vulgarity and noise. One immediate effect of an influx of motorists, as opposed to those who spend their holidays in the mountains for the sake of peace and quietness, is on the economic and social life of a small community. The peasant, who previously lived simply and happily is apt to become cunning and discontented when absorbed by civilisation. Catchpenny phrases such as "standard of living" engage his attention, and he presently becomes imbued with that restless kind of striving after an ephemeral "something," which characterises those who live and work in cities, without realising that in so doing he is jettisoning contentment and happiness. An Alpine village which is being "developed" by motor-car and tourist would make an interesting sociological study.

La Bérarde is an example of an essentially primitive Alpine hamlet that is being rapidly "developed" by tourism. There is one comparatively new hotel, a pleasant structure built in the chalet tradition; for the rest the village houses have been converted into (it would be more truthful to say have become) hotels, whilst there is, of course, the inevitable shop selling picture postcards and trinkets, the trashy nature of which bears testimony to the type of mind that purchases them, and the decline of art in general. At frequent intervals cars and charabancs arrive; they disgorge their passengers who, after refreshing themselves at one or other of the hotels, walk a few hundred yards (the more energetic among them), buy postcards and trinkets (made anywhere but in Dauphiné), and depart in a cloud of dust, happily conscious that they have "done" the Central Alps of Dauphiné, a fortunate illusion which no true lover of that country would want to dispel.

After lunch, we shouldered our rucksacks and set off to the Alp de Carrelet and our bivouac place. The weather was now perfect, and after the usual pause for refreshment at the Carrelet hut we mounted leisurely through a forest of small pines towards the site of the Temple-Ecrins hut.

It was a pleasant walk, and we paused more than once to contemplate the beauty of the view, which included Les Bans set gracefully at the head of the curving Pilatte glacier, and the abrupt rocky pile of the Pic Coolidge, a peak Dolomitic in aspect by virtue of its yellowish colour and formidable appearance.

As we neared the limit of the forest we cast around for a bivouac site, but, as there was no level place, continued, until we were above the forest and on open ground below the Temple-Ecrins hut. Here we came upon some almost level turf, complete with a small stream and, best of all, a quantity of firewood in the shape of the remains of the former hut which had been swept down by the avalanche. In Scotland or Switzerland we might have entertained doubts as to the legality of burning even the debris of a hut, but we felt that there was unlikely to be any officious person in the vicinity, and that no one would worry over the destruction of a few planks.

In order to save weight we had left our sleeping-bags at La Bérarde and had brought with us only the tent. This we erected, and uncomfortably low it seemed when the two supporting ice axes had been affixed to either end. However, we consoled ourselves with the thought that we should start shortly after midnight.

The sun set soon after our arrival, but we counteracted the chill that came quickly to the air with a roaring fire of hut debris. "It is," as Jim remarked, "an ill avalanche that blows nobody any wood."

The evening was serenely calm. During the day, cumulus clouds, the products of moist valley air, had gathered about the mountains, but towards sundown they began slowly to break up, until only a few thin wisps were left, a delicate pastel pink, against a green sky. The most striking object in view was the Pointe du Vallon des Etages in the south-west, a peak bearing a striking resemblance to the Matterhorn. Eastwards, the topmost crags of the Ecrins were visible, glowing in the sun's last rays. The stars waxed gradually brighter and the light from our fire grew on the gentian-carpeted turf.

Many a time I have pondered over the peace and tranquillity of the hills. It seems that man when he treads the city street treads some lower spiritual level and that on the hills he meets with something better than the mere negation of noise and haste. There is spiritually a positive quality about Nature, just as there is a negative quality about the centres of civilisation. The artificial and the superficial tend to promote evil rather than good; the natural, though it may be disregardful of life, is essentially good because it teaches restless, striving, and unhappy man the virtues of order, rhythm, and tranquillity. Nature seldom takes life except to perpetuate her species, whereas men take life for motives of anger, greed, power, selfishness, and jealousy. There seems inherent in hills a Presence of Peace, and this Presence is perceptible to those who listen with all ears. To the true philosopher Peace is discernible anywhere, but for most men this is impossible because of their physical environment, and they must seek it in quiet places far removed from the activities of their fellows. It is from this lower grade that the hermit, the monk, and the nun come. Theirs is a confession that they have failed to find spiritual peace, because of their own incapacity to do so. They are afraid to face up to the problem of finding it in the company of their fellow men, and prefer to seek peace rather than to make it.

The modern escapist is in temperament and desire something between the peace finder and the peace maker. He seldom understands his own motives; in his desire to escape for a while from the noise and confinement of the city he accedes to a blind and sometimes selfish instinct. He may delude himself with talk of sunlight, hard exercise, and fresh air, but the real reason for his escape is a search for peace. Peace is the natural, not the unnatural, end of human progress, and its evolution is to be discerned not only in Geneva and the correspondence columns of newspapers, but in the heart of every man who seeks the solace of a quiet and restful hour, and in every man whose scale of values is not rooted in a purely material conception of life.

The escapist is a glowing spark from the anvil where man is being forged. Perhaps decades hence a race, living let us hope in amity amid beautiful surroundings, will examine critically present-day man's spiritual yearning for a peace of mind and body that at the moment of writing seems as far out of his reach as ever. They will discern a growing revolt against ugliness, and social and economic misery, and the dawn of a new era, the beginning perhaps of a Romantic Age in which beauty and the creation of beauty will find a new scope and a new recognition.

If the mountains do nothing else they at least tend to promote thought, for only the fool or the dullard can stand on a high hill without sensing a destiny and a peace in which earthly death is the merest incidental.

Darkness was gathering as we prepared and ate our supper. This, as at first planned, was to be a single course of soup with trimmings, but Jim presently remembered that among our provisions were some dried apricots and suggested that these might be improved and rendered succulent by immersion in boiling water. This was no sooner said than done and our aluminium pan was placed over the fire on two stones so arranged as to form a small trench. All went well until the pan was retrieved from the fire. Jim did this, but it was a delicate operation as the pan had no handle, and in the middle of it something went wrong and our precious sweet was distributed over the grass and among the ashes of the fire. Jim was deeply chagrined, and on several subsequent occasions referred to the incident in scathing self-condemnatory terms. Fortunately the damage was largely repaired by our scooping up the apricots and eating them; they were pronounced to be excellent, in spite of ashes and other foreign matter adhering to them.

By the time we had eaten our supper, darkness had completely fallen. We piled wood on to the fire and sat by a great blaze smoking our pipes; and a pipe never tastes so good as when it is smoked in the open by a wood fire. As we sat we talked. I asked Jim whether younger officers in the army still cherished illusions as to the manner and meaning of war. His reply was that none, not even those too young to remember the last war, had any illusions, war was an unpleasant and bloody business.

At that moment the thought of war seemed unreal

and fantastic. The moon was rising behind the Ecrins and its rays shone on the rock peaks opposite to us across the valley. One great lesson Nature has to teach man is methodicity. On mountains the rhythm of the universe is appreciated more easily than it is at lower levels. From the high and lonely outposts of the earth the mountaineer gazes with humble awe outwards and beyond the hilltops into space. And as he gazes he senses an answer to the meaning of life. He looks down dispassionately upon human strugglings and sufferings, yet knows full well that presently he must descend among them, taking his part in the world of men and affairs. Yet when he does so he carries down with him, as a pilgrim might who visits a shrine, a measure of the peace and serenity of spirit he has gained on the hills. He appreciates better the value of the essential, and the valuelessness of the unessential. Nature has taught him contentment and simplicity, that to overburden the mind with material matters is to incur discontentment, complexity, and unhappiness, that some detachment of mind and spirit in the midst of everyday affairs is the keystone of genuine happiness. He is able to appreciate the value of meditation and the dangers inherent in the spiritual quagmires of rush and speed, for speed more than anything else is synonymous with selfishness, callousness, and inconsiderateness. Thank God, machines are seldom seen on mountains. The Tibetans believe that to dig for minerals is to let loose devils. They have good cause to do so if it be remembered that the aeroplanes now raining destruction upon men are made from minerals dug out of the ground. Love of Nature is man's spiritual armour against the Moloch of the Machine. Through his sense of beauty in natural things he struggles to escape from a self-constituted and self-imposed enslavement. Nazi Germany is symptomatic of a spiritual enslavement. We are fighting to control materialism and its spawn, the machine.

Soon after moonrise, mists gathered above and below. This was due to a sudden lowering of temperature and presently, when equilibrium was established in the atmosphere, they dispersed and the peaks shone out clear and unclouded. The cold increased quickly and we were soon reduced to that state, which visitors to the average English hotel will readily recognise, of being scorched by an open fire from the front and withered by a cold draught from the rear.

Shortly after ten o'clock, we decided to seek refuge in our tent and try to sleep a little. As it seemed likely that the one farthest from the entrance would be asphyxiated during the night, we tossed for the privilege of outside berth. I won, and Jim had to take the risk.

Having insinuated ourselves through the small sleeve opening we lay down side by side. We had previously prepared a platform for the floor and this proved moderately comfortable, but because of the close confinement and lack of ventilation we found it impossible to sleep, and soon came to the conclusion that although the tent might prove its value in an emergency, it was otherwise to be avoided. Jim was the first to rebel and announced his intention of spending the remainder of the night by the fire. I was glad to follow suit, and we remade the fire and settled down as near to it as we dared, now and again turning our backs to the blaze, in the manner of grilling chops. So the night passed. We nodded and drowsed, and alternated between being roasted and frozen. Tent and turf were white with frost when at half-past two we stiffly roused ourselves to prepare our breakfast. Hot tea put fresh life into us, and an hour later we packed up the frost-stiffened tent and set out for our climb.

The night was cloudless, and as we breasted the slopes above our bivouac we saw before us the summit crags of the Ecrins bathed in the moonlight, floating like some ghostly vision in the stars.

For a while we trudged over loose stones, but presently came to a path zigzagging up the slopes between the glacier and the Pic Coolidge. The excellent state of this path proved that the ascent of the Ecrins from this direction is popular among climbers. Following a path uphill is a good preliminary to a day's mountaineering. It needs no skill and little effort, yet the exercise is sufficient to loosen the muscles, quicken the blood in the veins, and in general prepare the mountaineer for the more serious work of the day.

Dawn came as we passed beneath the ferocious northwest precipice of the Pic Coolidge. Slowly the shadows cast by the waning moon were absorbed by the increasing light. It was a glorious morning. For some time past, as we had mounted the path, I had speculated half sleepily as to the nature of a luminous white

4

cloud hovering in the north-western sky, but as the light grew I saw that it was the great snow-field of Les Rouies.

Daylight came as we trod the frozen surface of the glacier. We had to pass beneath the mouths of some stone-swept couloirs falling from the Pic Coolidge, but at that hour the mountain artillery was silent and nothing fell. A little later we crossed the southernmost branch of the glacier and mounted some rocks to the northernmost branch which ends in the Col des Avalanches under the south wall of the Ecrins. We already knew that there were others ahead of us, and as we turned a corner and came within sight of the cliffs of the Ecrins, we saw and heard two parties, the first of two, and the second of four men. They were already on the rocks, and must have started at least an hour before us, after sleeping in the half-built hut. This was annoying, as we realised that it would be inadvisable to follow them for some time owing to stones they might knock down on us. We decided, therefore, to mount to the Col des Avalanches, find some spot out of reach of a light but bitterly cold wind, and breakfast. This decision was soon proved to be right as presently we heard excited shouts and the rattling of stones.

We had no difficulty in reaching the col but to descend on the other side of it out of the wind was a different matter. Shivering in an icy blast we gazed down a sheer precipice falling for many hundreds of feet into an icy stone-scarred gully, descending with terrific steepness some 3,000 feet to the Glacier Noir. There was, however,

one ledge which appeared large enough for our purpose
and, while Jim held me on the rope, I descended from the
ridge to investigate it. It proved to be only two feet in
breadth; I edged and shuffled along it, but had not gone
far when I realised that it was by no means safe. The rocks
above and below were unstable and I could feel the whole
mountain-side tremble slightly, or so I imagined. I was
about to retrace my steps when out of the corner of my
eye I saw a patch of blue. It was a cushion of the Alpine
forget-me-not (*Eritrichium nanum*), and near it were
growing other cushions covered with stemless blue
flowers, a blue matching the sky and, in brilliance and
purity, seeming to partake of the very atmosphere. Here
was an example of Nature's adaptation to circumstances,
for the Col des Avalanches is 11,515 feet above the sea.
These little plants had weathered and endured countless
storms and freezing cold, yet in their close-packed
foliage, set tightly and snugly in niches and crannies of
the rocks, was the will and the capacity to exist and to
endure.

I rejoined Jim and we decided to wait at the foot of the
rocks on which the other two parties were climbing. As
we approached the rocks we heard warning shouts and
then the whizz of stones. We made haste to make ourselves as small as possible under a vertical wall, and there
we had to remain for the next hour or more. It was a
depressing situation for, if we were safe from stones, we
were assaulted by the bitterly cold wind and were in
shadow out of the sun, which shone, as it seemed to us,
with fulsome self-esteem on the cliffs of the Fifre, a peak

of 12,075 feet to the south of the Col des Avalanches. How we longed for its warmth as we beat and kicked our hands and feet together, while listening to the humming and whining of the stones dislodged every few seconds by those above us. Why couldn't the two parties get a move on? we asked ourselves time and again. What the deuce were they doing? We could hear their voices, but presently they ceased and with them the stone-falls. I ventured forth from the protective rocks, and gazed up the gully to the left. I was about to tell Jim that it was safe to advance when once again came the rattling of stones and I just had time to scurry back like a rabbit into its burrow when down they came with a vicious clatter, clatter, and whizz, whizz, flying and ricochetting like bullets.

There was another long and disagreeable wait, but at length it seemed that the stones really had ceased to fall and gingerly we forsook our shelter and, with many an anxious glance upwards, proceeded to follow tracks in the snow up the gully to our left. This divided above into two chimneys. The right hand of these was glazed with ice and looked so repulsive that we decided that the left-hand one was the route of ascent. In deciding this we made our first blunder. As was obvious from the tracks in the snow, the other parties ahead of us had attempted the same route and we assumed, with what justification I do not know, that they knew the way. In point of fact, they knew it no better than we, and we were led into an impossibly difficult chimney. We retreated, baffled. As already mentioned the right hand of the two chimneys looked equally unattractive, and to avoid it we attempted to scale the rocks to one side of it. Our manoeuvres were so varied and complicated that I am entirely unable to remember them in detail. I have a vague recollection of climbing some steep and difficult rocks to the left of the ice-glazed chimney and of trying to traverse into the latter above the icy section. This failed and, eventually, after over an hour's work, we retired to the snow, where we indulged in a good grouse against everyone and everything, excluding, of course, ourselves who were really to blame. I will spare the epithets, and economise in the asterisks, and will only remark that the things we had to say about the parties in front of us were excusable having regard to the provoking circumstances.

Were we to be beaten before we had begun? Were we to creep ignominiously back to our bivouac place and La Bérarde? It was not to be contemplated for a moment. Get up we would, come what might. "I am sure the route must lie up that chimney," said Jim, pointing to the unpleasant ice-glazed rift already mentioned. "The guide-book says . . ." But we had already read our fill of the guide-book, and had come to the conclusion that it was wrong in every particular. "I'm going to try it," continued Jim imperturbably, in response to my growl of scepticism, and without further ado, he set about wrestling with the intricacies of the cleft. And he *did* do it. It was a good lead, and he had to surmount one particularly wicked bit some distance up. The chimney was long, but proved easier than anticipated; it is probably not difficult in normal conditions; but the presence of ice may turn the easiest route into a struggle, and we realised as we mounted one reason for the slow progress of the parties in front of us.

The chimney slanted from left to right across the face of the mountain. It provided a sufficiency of resting-places, and Jim seldom had to run out more than fifty or sixty feet of rope. He was in good form and climbed confidently and well, but I was the reverse and put up a sorry performance on the cold ice-sheeted rocks. It is worse than disagreeable climbing steep rocks when you are out of form; physical unfitness interposes a barrier between the climber and the mountain so that the latter seems remote and hostile. In such circumstances climbing is the reverse of enjoyable; it approaches too near to the border-line of fear. Climbing when in good form is a very different matter. There is no physical or psychological barrier between man and mountain. There is no "dithering", no indecision, no vacillation; calmness, confidence, and enjoyment are experienced by the climber, who is physically and mentally fit; there is harmony. This applies to most forms of human activity. It is no good trying to do a job of work for which there is not the requisite knowledge, skill, and capacity. The work retaliates on the worker. So it is in mountaineering, as the annual accidents list reveals. Mountains are apt to retaliate on those who approach them without skill, knowledge, and humility.

The chimney petered out into debris-covered rocks and patches of snow. We paused and searched the cliffs ahead of us. The guide-book said that it was necessary to bear

to the right, then mount some difficult rocks by means
of a fixed cable. The route, however, was not visible.
Immediately above us was a deeply cut snow-filled gully,
ending in sheer overhanging precipices. There was no
way here that we could see, and in any event to mount
directly upwards seemed contrary to the instructions of
the guide-book; nor could we see any sign of the parties
ahead of us.

I suggested to Jim that we must look to the right and
that I would go ahead and prospect. He agreed, and I set
off up some slabby rocks to one side of a shallow scoop.
Here and there these rocks appeared scratched as though
by bootnails, but there was otherwise no definite indica-
tion of a route in this direction. A long wait at the foot of
the precipice had chilled us to the bone, and climbing the
icy chimney in the shadow had done little to improve our
condition. But now we were in the sun and the rocks
were warming every instant. For the first time that day
I began to extract some pleasure from the climbing. It
was a sensational position in which I found myself after
an ascent of some forty or fifty feet. Immediately above
me was a thin chimney, a ferocious overhanging rift,
with some loose rocks wedged insecurely in its uppermost portion. Surely the route could not lie there;
the difficulties were as obvious as they were desperate.
On both sides of the chimney the cliffs were patently
unassailable, vertical or overhanging walls of yellowish
rock. Was there a route still farther to the right? If so, it
could only be gained by traversing at a lower level. I
decided to investigate and commenced to descend some

steep rocks which formed the left-hand wall of the chimney, my plan being to cross the latter lower down, turn a rock nose and examine what lay beyond. Before doing this I brought up Jim, so that I was well held from above. It was an awkward descent; the rocks were not sound, and I had to test every hold; the precipice below was abysmal.

Thirty or forty feet lower I became convinced that we were hopelessly off the route. The proposed traverse across the chimney to the right was as difficult as it was dangerous, and I knew that neither extreme difficulty nor danger are met with on the south face of the Ecrins if the proper route is followed. So I shouted up to Jim, "It's no good, I don't think we can get round there, it's a horrible place. We had better get back. I can traverse from here," to which he replied cheerfully, "All right, I'm not very well placed but I can hold you."

A nearly horizontal traverse was the shortest way back to the point from which we had started, but it was undoubtedly "thin" and exposed, the holds being small, and I was glad to regain the debris-covered rocks. Jim returned by my route of ascent and presently we were reunited. More than an hour had passed and we were no wiser than before.

Our next move was to attempt a traverse at a lower level; but this proved equally futile. We found ourselves on treacherously loose rocks of tremendous steepness and were glad to beat a retreat. Two hours had now passed and time was galloping. If we did not at once find a route we should have to retreat. We were puzzled and angry with the guide-book and with ourselves. We had seen some steps in a patch of snow near the mouth of the "impossible" gully, but had dismissed the latter out of hand. Could it be that the route followed this gully despite all appearances to the contrary? Was it a case of the "second degree". We had been misled by our predecessors at the commencement of the climb and had believed, when we saw their traces the second time, that we should be misled again if we followed them, especially in view of the apparent impossibility of climbing the gully. Was it possible that on this occasion they were right, and that we must follow the evil-looking rift?

At this point in our dilemma we heard voices, and next moment the familiar rattling of stones, a few of which came flying past us out of the mouth of the gully. We beat a hasty retreat, then paused and looked up. The problem was immediately solved when we saw three figures descending a fixed cable into the gully from the rocks to the right of it. The cable was obviously that mentioned in the guide-book. But why was the party descending? What had gone wrong? These questions could only be solved by personal contact. At all events, there was the route plain to see, and we were going to climb it.

Shouting up a warning that we were in the line of fire from stones, we rapidly climbed up into the mouth of the gully. As we did so, doubt and indecision vanished like snowflakes in the sun. We had been tricked and bamboozled; our blood was up; for the first time that day we climbed quickly and confidently.

Soon we were at the point where it was necessary to leave the gully in favour of the rocks to the right. Down these rocks extended a stout steel cable attached at intervals to iron spikes. Three Frenchmen were descending it. They were painfully slow and for some inscrutable reason were using a doubled rope in addition to the cable. It was no use waiting for them. They would take half an hour at least to get down, and we set off up the cable.

Climbing which entails mere gymnastic strength and agility is not the most enjoyable kind of climbing, and ascents such as the Dent du Géant and the Italian side of the Matterhorn, where hundreds of feet of fixed ropes or cables must be scaled, are more strenuous than meritorious or pleasurable from a mountaineering standpoint. Not only is such climbing artificial, but there is always the disquieting thought at the back of the mind that perhaps the ropes or cables are insecurely attached or have rotted or rusted away. On this section of the Ecrins, the rocks are less difficult than those we had been climbing in our attempt to discover the route, and the cable is therefore unnecessary. Time, however, was now of such vital consequence that we did not hesitate to shin up as quickly as possible. *En route* we passed the three retreating climbers and asked them why they had abandoned the climb. Their disconsolate and scarcely encouraging reply was, "We lost the way and we are too slow," an inadequate explanation in view of the fact that they were climbing behind another party who had not retreated, having apparently found the route. I fear that we did not feel charitably disposed towards them, for we had spent much time in dodging the stones they had knocked down; also it was their initial blunder that had led to so much wastage of time. On a complicated mountain-side like the south face of the Ecrins, it is unwise to assume that a party in front of you is right or wrong unless it is known to be accompanied by someone who knows the route. Failing such knowledge he is a wise mountaineer who adheres unswervingly to his own judgment.

Above the fixed cable were some steep but comparatively easy rocks. These brought us to a corner and an incipient ice-filled gully which we crossed to a rocky rib. And here again we went wrong. We should, I believe, have made a further traverse to the right, but we elected to climb directly upwards. For a few feet the rocks were practicable, then they rose in an overhanging nose, which forced us back into the gully we had just crossed. At this point the gully was ice-filled and exceedingly steep for a few feet, but a little higher the ice gave place to rocks set at an even steeper angle, smooth slabby rocks, oozing with melted snow-water. We had both of us now completely recovered from our former despondency, and I, who was then in the lead, was feeling more energetic, yet, in my semi-trained condition, this section of the climb taxed me severely. The rocks showed no signs of nail marks, and it seemed certain that we were again off the route, but it was obvious that if they could be climbed we would gain easier ground above.

The holds were small, and few and far between; it was possible to get the first joint of the fingers and the tip of a boot on them and no more. An additional disadvantage was that Jim was some distance below, having secured himself to a belay on the easier rocks, there being no stance in the gully; thus a slip would have involved flying like a bullet from a gun down the icy gully, which in steepness and appearance resembled a frozen waterfall.

Climbing those wet slabs was a horrid experience. I was not at all sure of myself, and my movements were jerky. I put strength rather than skill into the work, as a climber does when he is not in training. The rocks were cold and wet, and I felt my finger-tips becoming numb. Half-way up it suddenly came to me that I should be hard put to it if I had to retreat. Had I the reserve strength? Perhaps I had; it is amazing how much strength a man can muster to meet real emergency; but at the time I felt that I had not; I felt that at any moment my legs would start that horrid uncontrollable trembling which arises simply and solely from lack of training. I have never fallen off rocks when leading a climb, but I understood then how and why this may happen. It may arise from lack of strength and skill, or from fear, or from a combination of all three, and it was from that detestable combination of weaknesses that I suffered on that occasion. Imagination can be a blessing and a curse on a mountain; it was a curse on that occasion. I pictured all too vividly the results of a slip: the slide with desperately grabbing hands down the rocks, the fearful velocity of the fall down the ice chute of the gully, the rope snapping on the belay like a piece of thread.

Jim had no inkling of my malaise, for he was in good training and came up like a bird. I remarked casually that I thought it was a bad place and he agreed. He complimented me on my lead, but I knew myself that I had climbed very badly. Had I failed to climb the last bit I might not have been able to retreat safely. I had taken a chance, and the chance had come off. But the fact that the chance had come off does not absolve me from a charge of reckless climbing and bad mountaineering.

We were now above the lower rock cliffs and on a great slope of snow set at a high angle, leading up for several hundred feet towards the crest of the Ecrins. The slope is intersected by various minor rocky ribs and we mounted by one of these without much difficulty, though the climbing was continuously steep. My memory, usually retentive of the details of a climb, is strangely vague as to this section of the route. What I do remember was an increasing anxiety as to the state of the weather. The early morning brilliance had been dimmed as we climbed, but so engrossed were we with the work that we scarcely noticed this. Now, as we toiled upwards, the sun disappeared behind formless grey mists drifting quickly out of the south-west. It was long past midday and it was necessary to hurry—above everything we must hurry.

There were rocks ahead, shattered crags ending in the summit ridge of the mountain, with little surges of mist moving along them like lazily propelled smoke.

Our rib ended and we had to ascend some snow diagonally to the right. There were steps here, evidently those of the party which had not turned back. Had the snow been in good condition we could have followed these steps and mounted over it most of the way to the summit ridge, but we were too late to do this; the snow was soft and concealed ice; to have climbed it much step cutting would have been necessary. So we took to the rocks on the right of the snow, loose, disagreeable rocks, yet safer and quicker than the snow. Up and up we progressed, rope length by rope length; extreme care was essential and every hold had to be tested.

The last bit was the best. Here the rocks, though steep, were firmer. The cliff ended with dramatic suddenness on the summit ridge. A strenuous scramble and we arrived there breathing hard, and with something more than a feeling of ordinary thankfulness.

We looked at our watches and were astonished to see that they registered 3.15 p.m. The climb had taken eight and three-quarter hours from the Col des Avalanches, of which three to four hours had been spent in waiting for the parties ahead and in finding the route. We vowed that it was the most complicated climb that we had ever done, and certainly I cannot recollect a climb of similar character in which so much time was spent in route finding. We had no cause for self-congratulation.

The actual summit of the Ecrins was a short distance to the east, but the lateness of the hour and the ominous weather made it imperative to descend immediately.

Before doing so, we paused for a few moments to take stock of our surroundings. Had it not been for the delays we should have enjoyed a magnificent panorama, but the brightness of the morning had gone out and the ranges loomed dull and indistinct beneath a lowering pall of slate-coloured cloud. As we stood, a few hailstones fell on the rocks at our feet with dry rustling whispers, and out of a still and silent void came a little wind that hissed a threatening whisper and was gone.

Our descent lay first of all over the Pic Lory, which is some sixty feet lower than the summit of the Ecrins, then down the ridge towards the Dôme de Neige, the route descended by Whymper's party in 1864. From Whymper's description, which was the only one I had read, I expected to find dangerously loose rock. Actually, the reverse was the case, and the passage of many climbers had deprived the route of ill-attached fragments, leaving a core of sound rock. There was no real difficulty in following the ridge, and we moved both together all the way, yet it was a beautiful and unique edge of rock, so thin in some places that it resembled a narrow wall splintered and breached by a cannonade.

For the most part we kept to the east side, and clambered along, holding on to the knife-like crest of the ridge with our hands. The climbing aroused all Jim's enthusiasm. "What a grand ridge!" he exclaimed on more than one occasion; and so it was, but like all grand things in life, it ended all too quickly, and we came to the point where a staircase cut out by the feet and axes of many climbers descended towards the Glacier Blanc. Down this we went without pause and, like Christian Almer seventy-five years before, found that the bergschrund at the foot of the slope could be jumped without difficulty.

Half an hour only had elapsed, and we lost no time in descending the upper slopes of the Glacier Blanc.

In order to reach the Col des Ecrins, we had to run the gauntlet of ice avalanches for a distance of about one hundred yards. Two had fallen and we lost no time in threading our way between the fallen blocks. We were soon out of range of the threatening masses of *séracs*, and trudged wearily through soft snow to the col. We had cheated the weather, but only just. As we stood on the col, we were enveloped by a thick drift of hail and a spiteful volleying wind; then from our left, high up amid the crags of the great peak from which we had descended, came a crackling growl of thunder.

The descent from the Col des Ecrins to the Glacier de la Bonne Pierre is simplified by the presence of numerous steel cables, and we devoutly hoped that the thunderstorm, raging on the Dôme de Neige immediately above us, would avoid our vicinity. The position of a climber who descends a wire cable on a mountain in a thunderstorm is analogous with that of a person who elects to scale a factory chimney in similar weather conditions by means of a lightning-conductor. However, any fears we might have entertained on this score were allayed, as the thunderstorm devoted itself exclusively to the Ecrins, doubtless under the mistaken belief that we were still on that mountain.

The descent was enlivened for me at one place by my ice axe doing its best to pitch me down the mountain-side. This occurred on the steepest section of the cable. I had put the axe through my waist loop of rope and, as I was shinning hand over hand down the cable, its point caught on a rock, so that for a short time I was unable to move either up or down, a disagreeable situation when the weight is dependent on the arms alone.

As we descended, we were interested and puzzled by the behaviour of two climbers on the snow slopes at the foot of the col. For a long time they were stationary, but at length succeeded in crossing the bergschrund on to the Glacier de la Bonne Pierre. The mystery was partly solved when we reached these slopes and saw the mark of an obvious, and unpremeditated, slide which ended on some rocks just above the bergschrund. The latter proved a formidable obstacle, but, after climbing down some rocks, we trod gingerly across a rickety-looking snow bridge spanning the gulf.

Snow was falling heavily as we slid and slithered down the upper slopes of the Glacier de la Bonne Pierre. Little was visible in the mist and gloom, but we followed the tracks of the two climbers we had seen and presently came up with them, two young Frenchmen who were sheltering from the snowstorm under a boulder. They generously offered us a drink of rum, which we gratefully accepted. Then they told us that one of them had slipped and fallen several hundred feet when they were climbing unroped down the slopes of the col. He had managed to stop himself at the rocks already mentioned a few yards short of the bergschrund. They had been the party in front of us all day, and it seemed strange that, having success- fully accomplished a difficult traverse, they should nearly come to grief on the easy slopes of the Col des Ecrins. But that is the way mountaineering accidents so often happen, when the difficulties are behind and easy climb- ing alone remains to be done. Reaction, inattention, care- lessness, these are the prime psychological causes of the great majority of Alpine disasters.

I do not know how or why the Glacier de la Bonne Pierre got its name; its moraines are not such as to merit this distinction, and a number of harsher terms occurred to us as we descended. But the merit of Dauphiné glaciers is that they are small, and their disagreeable features proportionately so; we emerged from the mist and snow and were soon in the valley that unites with the Etançons valley less than a mile from La Bérarde, the scanty pastures of which presently shone out from the rocky valley beneath.

Jim, true to that great British tradition of always descending from a mountain in time for table d'hôte, hastened on ahead with one of the Frenchmen, while I accompanied the other, a pleasant red-haired youth who talked so rapidly and so unintelligibly that I was content to reply, "Oui, Oui" or "Non, non" when an answer seemed indicated, a procedure which greatly impressed him with my conversational powers and knowledge of the French language.

What a delightful experience it is to descend from the high mountains after a hard day's climbing. One hour the mountaineer is among dead things, ice, snow, and rock, frozen, silent, and utterly indifferent to life, the next he is among life. First of all, he sees compact little plants set snugly in the stones of the moraine, anemones, saxifrages, drabas, and androsaces, their blooms silken and shining, then, as he descends, he enters into the kingdom of growing things. He sees water, that was higher frozen and silent, and hears the lilt and talk of it as it descends the hillside in rivulet and torrent, in ripple and rill, and glimmering pebble-floored pool. The air is soft, moist, and warm, not hard, dry, and cold, as it is on the heights, and charged with subtle and illusive fragrances, the smell of moist moss and herbage, the breath of flowers, warm resinous drifts from the pine-forest. To appreciate to the full this beauty of living things it is necessary to spend some weeks on the blizzard-swept slopes of a Himalayan peak, then to descend from the scorching sun glare, and the desiccating cold of flesh-shrivelling storms, to growing things. Never does the world seem so beautiful, and never is the meaning of life so evident, as it is at that glorious moment when the descending mountaineer first sees the starry blooms of a saxifrage or androsace peeping up at him from the stones of the moraine.

My companion presently wearied of a conversational monologue and at my frequent halts to examine flowers, and hastened on, leaving me to descend, as I always like to do, at my own slow pace.

Jim had good-naturedly waited for me and together we strolled through one or two little fields, almost ready to be cut for a second precious hay-crop, and re-entered La Bérarde, sixteen hours after we had set out that morning from our bivouac. We were well satisfied with a great day's mountaineering.

CHAPTER IV

INTERLUDE

THE morning after our traverse of the Ecrins we woke to find rain falling heavily and thunder reverberating from the heights. In the British hills, little account need be taken of rain; it is part and parcel of our soft island climate, and he is a faint-hearted climber who is deterred by it from making ascents. There is something stimulating rather than depressing about a rainy day on the Cumbrian fells. No clothing yet devised can prevent the walker or scrambler from becoming soaked to the skin; yet the antidotes, a hot bath, an open fire, a saddle of Herdwick mutton, and a glass of hot grog induce a feeling of well-being that must be experienced to be believed.

In the Alps, however, rain is a malefactor, an unwelcome intruder upon the domain of sun and blue sky, and it usually means snow on the mountains, which may rule out difficult ascents for a day or two after the weather has improved.

Alpine hotels are ill-adapted for rainy days. To an Englishman veal, veal, and yet more veal is a poor substitute for Welsh mutton or ribs of Scotch beef. There was not a hot bath to be had in the annexe of La Bérarde, whilst open fires and comfortable chairs are, of course, unheard of on the Continent. Much criticism has been levelled at the ghastly discomforts and horrible cooking of English hotels. It is the Englishman's privilege to criticise his own institutions, and he can do so without fear of incarceration in a concentration camp. The foreigner does not realise that such criticism is in ninety-nine cases out of a hundred a kind of inverted sentiment; therefore, he assumes that when a patriotic Englishman grumbles about his own institutions, those institutions must, in truth, be appalling. The Germans, more than any other people, are prone to make this psychological blunder; they have yet to learn that open grumbling and criticism are the hallmarks of Freedom and the guarantees of improvement. For myself, I have come to the conclusion, after travelling in various parts of the world, that there is no hotel quite so bad as a bad English hotel, and no hotel so good as a good English hotel.

During the two days that Jim and I were forced to remain inactive, we came very near to being bored. As both days were similar in their general characteristics, it is only necessary to describe one. We awoke and looked out of the window. Clouds were low on the mountains, and rain was falling steadily on to a tin roof with a depressing sound which reminded me of Somerset Maugham's play "Rain". One or two disconsolate tourists were standing about in the village street, clad in mackintoshes or capes, whilst the whitewashed houses, patched and streaked with damp, presented a somewhat debauched appearance. We dressed and came down to breakfast, banging our heads as usual against the floor of the landing as we descended the stairs, which had

apparently been constructed for the passage of persons
not exceeding five feet in height.

We entered the *salle-à-manger*, steeling ourselves to
resist unflinching an atmosphere that never knew an open
window, and was charged with the smell of stale tobacco
smoke, mingling with a curious and indescribable drift
from the kitchen, compounded apparently of dirty dish-
cloths, grease, smoke, garlic, coffee, and various unidenti-
fiable substances and liquids. Continuing to steel ourselves
we approached our table. On it we perceived the debris
of last night's supper, together with an ashtray piled with
cigarette-ends, the usual toothpicks and the usual tablecloth.

We took our seats and awaited the advent of "Jules".
We liked Jules and we felt sorry for him. He was always
working and always overworked, a satellite that revolved
unceasingly about Madame who seldom appeared to the
public gaze. Like the servitor of old, he went about his
duties in a waistcoat and shirt-sleeves with a green apron
tied to his waist. He was not above seventeen or eighteen
years of age, and he had a thin body and a thin, white face
surmounted by thin, lank, dark hair. In outward appearance he was always exactly the same, which suggested
that he never went to bed, or if he did go to bed had
no time to take off his clothes. He was a timid, friendly
fellow, and, as we felt instinctively, only existed to be
"put upon"; that is was a case of "Jules will do it", and
"Leave it to Jules". He was at once the "Bill" and the
"Smike" of the establishment.

Jules presently appeared and, having cleared the débris

of dinner away, but leaving the usual toothpicks and the usual tablecloth *in situ*, brought us a *café complet*, which, being interpreted, meant almost stone-cold coffee, and milk, topped with a dense skin of revolting appearance, thick crusty doorsteps of sour bread, pats of butter, which in taste and aroma suggested the goat, and a glutinous yellow substance which we agreed was probably apricot jam.

We shouted to Jules, and Jules reappeared. We mustered all the French at our command. Why was the coffee cold? It was disgusting. We sought for other and equally appropriate adjectives: and the milk: in future, a strainer must be provided to separate the liquid from the solid.

Up went Jules's shoulders and eyebrows in the expressive French manner, as much as to say, "These Englishmen, *parbleu*! They are particular. There is no satisfying them. Why cannot they be content with a crust of bread and a sip of coffee?"

He smiled bleakly. Yes, it was even as Monsieur said, the coffee *was* a trifle cold. It would be heated again, and if Monsieur desired to strain the milk, a strainer would be provided. Off he went, his mind dwelling on the curious idiosyncrasies of Englishmen, in particular their tendency to regard with disfavour skin on the milk, when other and more sensible people looked upon it as a delicacy, especially when spread upon bread.

A long interval, and the coffee reappeared, two or three degrees Fahrenheit warmer. Is the sour, hard, crusty bread, which it is necessary to tear like a wolf before it can be eaten, really palatable to Frenchmen? Presumably it is,

and that soft, fine-grained English bread is obnoxious to
a Frenchman. Tradition and custom are, of course, everything in the matter of food; I have given a Tibetan a tin
containing a choice product of Messrs Fortnum & Mason,
seen him make a wry expression, empty the contents
on to the ground and make off with the empty tin,
smiling happily. Yet it might be supposed that in
bread-eating countries there would be some common
standard.

During the morning we watched the rain falling, wrote
letters, and perused sundry magazines, deposited by
former travellers, of dentist waiting-room vintage. Lunch
was much better than breakfast, for the Frenchman's
appetite rouses itself by midday. During the afternoon we
saw various parties of tourists arrive in motor-cars and
charabancs. They alighted, ate a meal, stood about in
the rain for some minutes, then re-entered their vehicles
and departed. They had "done" La Bérarde and it is only
logical to assume that La Bérarde had "done" them. Why
they came to that village must remain a mystery, for
there was absolutely nothing to be seen except low clouds,
stony hillsides, and rain.

At the sacred hour of five o'clock we retired to our
bedroom, bumping our heads as usual during the ascent
of the stairs, and brewed some tea over our spirit cooker,
consoling ourselves still further with a home-made cake
that had accompanied us from England. Had it not been
for tea, we might well have embarked on some desperate
and lawless action, but it enabled us to maintain that
equanimity and contentment of spirit that is possible with

the Englishman who, though he may have lost all, yet still has his five-o'clock tea.

The second day was precisely similar to the first, except that the rain descended with ever greater ferocity, and the snow-line crept down to within 3,000 feet of the village. At the end of it, while we were eating the inevitable veal, Jim suddenly said, "What about the Pâtisserie des Alpes?" He referred to the well-known tea-room at Chamonix, and I was quick to catch his meaning.

"Right," I said, "we'll go to Chamonix to-morrow."

It was a grey, drizzling morning when we boarded the motor-bus for Grenoble. We felt rather like a man who, having been to the dentist and had one extraction, must needs return for another. We were relieved, however, to note that the bus was a modern and less decrepit vehicle than that which had transported us to La Bérarde. Also our former driver had been superseded by a tall, lean man with a long, thin, lantern-shaped face and prominent nose, who wore a beret cocked at a rakish and decisive angle and a cigarette, which he transferred from one corner of his mouth and back again with a single and miraculous facial contortion. We gazed at him earnestly, realising that upon him our safety depended. Here, we told ourselves, was the Frenchman of fact and fiction, the nonchalant Frenchman, magnificent in war, supreme in emergency, the Frenchman who drives a supercharged Bugatti round the Montlhéry circuit without turning a hair at a speed bordering upon the impossible.

He seemed unconscious of our scrutiny, and seated himself at the wheel with our former podgy driver at his side.

I have already exhausted my adjectives in describing the drive from Grenoble to La Bérarde and have none left for the return journey. I can only say that it was terrific, and that the driving would have prematurely whitened the hairs of Sir Malcolm Campbell. When we came, as we soon did, to the snake-like portion of the road, we rounded the corners by the simple process of skidding them, our wheels never more than a few inches from the edges of precipitous drops.

Our descent put me in mind of a story told about the late Sir Henry Segrave. He was given a bus to drive during the General Strike, but to his chagrin and disappointment, found that all he could get out of it was fifty-five miles an hour, to do which he put it in neutral on Hampstead Hill. It is said that he was surprised and pained when all the passengers got out at the first stop.

During the whole of this tremendous descent, our driver engaged in animated conversation with our ex-driver; and would now and again turn in his seat and pass some quip over his shoulder to the passengers, returning to his driving just in time to skid the next corner. I can still see the profile of his long, lean, melancholy Gallic countenance, engaged in the endless pursuit of transferring a cigarette stub from one corner of his mouth to the other, and feel the motor-coach rocking beneath me as it tore down the narrow mountain-road towards some corner skirting an abysmal drop round which it seemed humanly and mechanically impossible to go.

We arrived in safety at Le Bourg-d'Oisans. The worst was over and we regarded with neutral feelings a change of drivers, the bandit, as we called him, being replaced by the podgy man. After this, the wide Route des Alpes was a bagatelle and the seventy or eighty kilometres per hour with which we traversed it, a snail's crawl.

At Grenoble we had several hours to wait for the train and occupied ourselves with wandering about the town. It was Sunday and, although no Continental city can ever hope to emulate the awfulness of a London Sunday, Grenoble is imbued, in the morning at least, with a certain atmosphere of propriety; that is to say, some of the shops are shut; there are fewer passers-by in the streets than during weekdays; and many persons have seen fit to clad themselves in black clothing, a trait which the respectable French bourgeoisie share with the Swiss, in addition, of course, to the carrying of umbrellas.

From Grenoble we travelled to Chambery and Aix les Bains, and there changed into a train for Annecy. The bad weather seemed to be limited to the High Alps, for the weather in the foot-hill region was perfect. This last, as already mentioned, is an ideal country for a walking or camping tour, and I made a resolution to return one day to the Grande Chartreuse. When I am too old and feeble to scale high mountains, I shall be well content to gaze from a distance upon the snows, and wander amongst the green hills, the woods, and the flowers of the lower alps. In the first flush of youth, and in active middle age, it is not easy to picture physical feebleness and a curtailment of activity, yet the very nature of mountains helps to instruct a man in the art of living, which is to be spiritually contented. As the train lumped along towards Annecy I gazed up at the high green hills and tried to imagine myself years hence ensconced on one of their summits, gazing towards the distant snows. Even if I had not the strength to climb a low hill I should still go to the mountains, in order to be among them, and feel them about me as I have always known them. I should no longer know a fierce desire to grapple with rock, snow, and ice, but would be content merely to gaze upwards between the clouds at their precipices and their remote shining snow. No regretful or jealous pangs would be mine. Vision alone would content me. Physically, all I should ask for would be to feel the cool breath from the snows tempering the heat of the summer sun, to listen to the same glacier stream, to smell the same smells, of hushed pine forests, of warm shower-soaked turf, of flowers and fresh-cut hay. What matters age or feebleness when so much is left?

At Annecy, a clean, flourishing little town at the northernmost end of the lake of the same name, we gravitated automatically to a *pâtisserie*, and endeavoured, not without success, to compensate the inner man for the Spartan living imposed on him at La Bérarde.

Replete with ices of various flavours, and dangerous-looking pastries, we climbed into the motor-bus that was to convey us to Chamonix. We had become inured to French driving, and our progress on this occasion seemed devoid of excitement. It is true that Jim lost his hat over-board, and that we nearly crushed a corpulent old gentle-man in a straw hat against a wall, but the mere fact that we took corners fast and blind in the traditional French manner, seemed small beer after the Brooklands-cum-Montlhéry descent from La Bérarde.

How many centuries will elapse before man learns to be considerate to his fellow men when in charge of a vehicle? It would seem that speed and mechanisation have an adverse effect on the human intellect. Men and women, who are otherwise courteous, considerate, and kind, be-come rude, inconsiderate and utterly callous at the wheel of a motor-car. Why is this? What is the psychological explanation? Is speed a drug or a stimulant like morphia or cocaine, stifling the best and bringing out the worst in man? If so, the Church would do well to recognise the fact. A sermon on the sin of speeding would at least be stimulating and controversial, and a change from disserta-tions on other and more conventional forms of sin.

Lack of education and imagination is at the root of many evils. The man who drops a bomb from an aero-plane sees merely a blob of smoke on a large map, something so remote from his action that the two seem scarcely connected. In another minute or two, the smoke blob is far behind and out of sight. He has not the imagination to picture the damage and misery he is causing. Eliminate machines and explosives but leave civilisation in its same state in other respects, and it is doubtful whether war, if fought by cold steel alone, would be fought at all; its incongruousness would be brought home to man. The paradoxical thing about civilisation is that it has perpetuated the possibility of war through its creation of the machine, and precisely the same callousness that obtains on the roads of Europe to-day, makes possible the pressing of a button as a result of which men are killed and maimed miles away. If education is to be effective, it must above all things cultivate imagination in youth, for without imagination, the possibility of waging war, which will become easier as machines are improved, will only increase. In the meantime, the psychology of speed, and the relationship between man and machine, provides a study for the best brains of the age, for if man is allowed to speed unchecked on his mad rush he must head for destruction. *Diabolo ex machina.*

The Lake of Annecy is a favourite rendezvous of French people from Lyon, and other cities, and its banks presented a gay spectacle this sunny afternoon. After passing the lake, the road mounted through a forest to the village of Ugines, then followed the Arly Valley to Mégève. At one village, I forget which, we stopped, in order to allow the passengers to visit some gorge, waterfall, or other natural attraction. Jim and I meanwhile enjoyed a drink, and agreed over it that organised sight-seeing was not for us. Why was this? Was it mere superiority on our part that prevented us from jostling along with a crowd of other people to gape and stare at some waterfall or fairy-glen (admission two francs), or was it boredom, or some other horrible human characteristic? I have often asked myself why I dislike "sights", why I detest accompanying a crowd of goggling and gaping trippers, and listening to a raucous-voiced guide, expatiating on the merits, beauties, and historical interests of the said "sights". A star in Baedeker is sufficient to send me post-haste in the opposite direction, except, of course, in the matter of hotels.

For me Nature when commercialised, becomes dull and tedious to witness. Turnstiles and a fairy-glen are incompatible associates, and even a high and magnificent waterfall becomes a sad, shamefaced affair when viewed from behind an iron railing with a row of parked charabancs in the background. Beauty and grandeur in nature lie primarily in exclusiveness, remoteness, and unexpectedness. A countryside is infinitely more alluring when you have not read about it in guide-books, and told which parts of it are admirable and which are not. Even in mountaineering I regard guide-books with a certain hostility and innate suspicion. I do not want to be told where to climb and how to climb. I want to climb and find out things for myself; it is much better fun and, incidentally, better mountaineering.

Continuing on our way, we passed through Mégève. Not so very many years ago, I spent a night at an inn in this village, a simple charming inn, where I was entertained by some strolling minstrels. Mégève then was a sleepy little village of no particular importance, but it has since become a fashionable winter sports resort. It is unjust to condemn a place merely because it has become popular and been transformed from a village into a "resort", yet I can never repress a certain feeling of sadness when I see an Alpine village that I had formerly known as simple, "old world", and primitive, "discovered" by the outside world and transformed into a venue for film stars. However skilfully this transformation may be effected, it reflects industrialism and all that industrialism means when applied to Nature. Private enterprise more often than not produces architectural uglinesses. Only socialisation in its best sense is going to save Nature from spoliation, for to money-grubbing man left to his own devices beauty in Nature means little or nothing. I was glad when Mégève was behind, and its barren piles of hotels, cable railways, and other appurtenances of tourism out of sight.

As we approached St. Gervais, we had to join a queue of vehicles, whose progress had been blocked for some unexplained reason. The motoring temperament reacts in a curious manner to an obstruction on the road, and the immediate Latin reaction is to press the horn and keep it going. I once worked in an office above the principal thoroughfare of Buenos Aires. Near-by was a cross-road, and when the policeman held up traffic, every motorist when his car came to a halt proceeded to blow his horn until the policeman lowered his hand. The noise was terrific and interfered considerably with business in the neighbouring blocks, yet it had come to be regarded as a custom of the country. It may be that to a citizen of Buenos Aires the failure of motor-drivers to blow their horns in a London traffic block is equally inexplicable.

It was evening as we entered the Arve Valley and approached Chamonix. Over the foothills the sky was clear, but Mont Blanc was concealed behind mists, yet, as we turned a corner, there came into sight a point of radiant sunlit snow. It was so high that the neck had to be craned to look at it, and seen through the misty window it appeared unearthly and unreal. What is the spell of a mountain-top that it should cause men and women to rise electrified in their seats and exclaim, "Wunderschön!" "Magnifique!" or "Wonderful!" according to their kind? Is it mere size? Is it colour? Is it shape? Is it remoteness? What link was there between that shining point and human emotion? Do men perceive through a high hill, through physical form and outward appearance, an all-pervading spiritual force?

Beneath Mont Blanc on the hem of its robing forests lies Chamonix. For me this place epitomises more than any place I know among mountains, the vulgarity of man. What is vulgarity in the mountains? It is not merely some effect produced by a large number of persons congregated together, it is not merely noise, untidiness, or architectural monstrosity; it is incompatibility, incongruity. Nothing is ugly except as a combination or a relationship with surrounding objects. Chamonix does not harmonise with its surroundings, nor for that matter does any city. But there are degrees of harmony, and standards which by custom come to be accepted, and Chamonix, I think, outrages these standards. The Alpine village before the advent of tourism became through custom and tradition an accepted, and therefore harmonious part, of the Alpine scene. This was due to centuries of slow growth and development, in which the prevailing motif was a profound conservatism. An Alpine village has not sprung up in a year, or in a decade; it has grown slowly. Tourism is a recent product and its growths are mushroomlike. Architecturally, it all too often outrages tradition, and produces in the minds of those who respect tradition a reaction of ugliness. This applies in smaller or greater degree to all Alpine villages that have been developed as tourist centres, though there are places in Switzerland or Austria where an honest attempt has been made to perpetuate tradition outwardly, while abandoning it inwardly for modern requirements in the matter of comfort, sanitation, etc. No such attempt has been made at Chamonix. It would appear that the private property owner and the city dweller who know nothing of Alpine architectural tradition are allowed full scope for their money-making propensities. That is the tragedy of Chamonix, and it is the tragedy of much of Europe. Mankind pays for the democratic system with ugliness, and will continue to pay so long as that system in its present form survives, so long as individual greed is allowed to trample upon public interest. It will occur under a socialist régime, and indeed under any régime so long as commercialism is considered to be of more importance than the preservation or construction of beautiful things.

Chamonix was crowded, but we managed to obtain accommodation at the Hôtel des Etrangers near the station, the cleanliness and good food of which contrasted agreeably with the annexe of La Bérarde, this being due to an enterprising proprietor, who spoke excellent English, an acquirement which in most Alpine hotels is usually responsible for a substantial bill.

That evening we amused ourselves by visiting a variety entertainment at the Casino, where we heard a number of comic songs, which we did not understand, and witnessed some convincing trouser-pulling.

Further, to improve our knowledge of the night life of Chamonix, we took a peep at the gambling where that depressing game of chance called Boule is played, depressing because there is even less chance of winning than there is at roulette and because gambling is, like alcohol, essentially a depressant in the long run.

Next we dived down for five minutes to an underground dance hall to emerge with smoke-smartened eyes into the starry night. As we agreed, night life is all very well in Paris or London, but it is out of place at Chamonix under the snows of Mont Blanc, at all events to the conservative mountaineer.

We had previously planned to climb one or more of the great routes on the south side of Mont Blanc, but these ascents demand perfect weather and conditions, and the weather was now unsettled. So we pored over the maps and eventually I suggested that we should postpone crossing the range into Italy and visit its western extremity which neither of us had seen.

The best centre for climbing hereabouts is the Trélatête Hotel, situated at the end of the glacier of the same name at a height of 6,450 feet, and enquiries elicited the fact that it was clean and comfortable. Should the weather improve we agreed that it would be good fun to traverse

Mont Blanc from this hotel and descend to Courmayeur in Italy, thence returning to Chamonix over the mountain by one of the southern routes.

This decided upon, we spent the morning after our arrival at Chamonix purchasing provisions, and shortly after midday boarded the motor-bus to Les Contamines and Notre-Dame-de-la-Gorge.

The drive was a pleasant experience and unaccompanied by excessive speed or reckless cornering. Although it was a grey day with a sullen cloud roof, the bus was crowded with tourists who obviously extracted plenty of enjoyment out of the ride in spite of the depressing weather. It is, of course, usual with that haughty and aloof person the mountaineer, to scorn and deride the foibles, eccentricities, and naïveties of the tourist. There is without doubt a certain insincerity about the "Wunderbars" and "Magnifiques" with which the tourist greets the Alpine glow and other phenomena, and the impact of such a chorus upon the splendour of Nature is to create an atmosphere of vulgarity, so that even the Alpine glow is relegated to the status of a picture postcard. A crowd of human beings and the sublimities of Nature simply do not mix; there is something aesthetically and spiritually wrong just as there is in a mixture of vintage port and Scotch whisky. For me it is impossible to enjoy natural scenery in the company of a number of my fellow men, and this prejudice applies to mountaineers as a whole. There is something essentially individualistic in man's relationship with, and appreciation of, Nature. Yet the mountaineer who sneers at the herds of tourists lays himself open to the charges of snobbery and intolerance. Far better if he sees in the rowdiest of paper-strewing picnic parties a glimmering of an idea that may eventually emancipate mankind from the purely materialistic conception.

It may be that some who visit Nature's sanctuaries do so merely because it is fashionable; that is the lowest and most ignorant form of travel, degrading to the finer sensibilities and destructive of those powers of self-determination and discrimination which separate mankind from the beast. But the great majority of those who spend their holidays in the mountains, whether singly or in groups, do so because they extract a genuine enjoyment from natural scenery. Their sentiments may seem cheap and stereotyped, and they never stop to question themselves as to why they enjoy this or that; their manners are sometimes abominable, and they strew their sandwich papers about the landscape, yet, though they do not realise it, they are responding automatically and without thought to the immemorial call of Nature: they are escaping from something which they cannot define, not merely bricks and mortar, smoke, and noise, but something artificial, and at variance with man's natural heritage which is Nature and the fruits of Nature. Will this revolt lead eventually to a decentralisation of mankind? Ages hence, will the inhabitants of this planet look back upon this age as an age of material enslavement? Will they see in its wars and tyrannies, in its economic miseries, the by-products of a strangling material existence into which even the sun is denied an entry?

Industrial centralisation and the manner in which it has been carried out without regard for the spiritual, mental, and physical well-being of man, was the danger of the nineteenth century and is the curse of the twentieth century. These tourists who escape from it for a week or two in every fifty-two weeks are the pioneers of a new decade in which art, literature, and knowledge will enrich the human mind.

Bigotry is not the least of human failings. Merely to climb mountains is not to enjoy mountains. There was more than a germ of truth in Ruskin's contention that mountaineers regarded mountains as greasy poles, for some mountaineers do regard mountains in this light; they see in Nature only a field of physical endeavour; mountain summits to them have the same worth as scalps to a Red Indian; they are concerned only with their own wretched feats and their superiority through muscular strength and skill over the tourist who is content to crawl about the lower slopes; yet, they are escapists, too, driven by some subconscious urge from the city into the open air and the sunlight. My own experience, included in which is public lecturing on mountaineering subjects, goes to show that there are more people outside the trade unionism of mountaineering, who extract a genuine spiritual enjoyment and inspiration from the mere presence of mountains and from being among mountains, than there are in that trade unionism. All too frequently, the sport of mountaineering tends to destroy the love of mountains. This may seem paradoxical, but I believe it is true. It may be argued in defence of mountaineers that they are inarticulate, yet even this cannot wholly explain the appalling literary mediocrity of climbing-club publications, and the predominance of the objective over the subjective. Of all God's creatures, the mountaineer who describes his climb in a mountaineering publication is in many ways the most stereotyped. If he feels anything he is afraid to express it. His horror of sentiment would be laughable were it not tragic. He is a slave to fashion. His descriptions are merely so many permutations and combinations of facts and observations. Above all, he gives the reader the impression of a fatuous and dreadful self-complacency. Perhaps he assumes that what he has seen and what he has felt has been seen so often and felt so often before by other people that any attempt at description is unnecessary. If so, this is a lazy habit of thought, a negation of individualism and a moral cowardice; the man who shrinks from expressing his thoughts and sentiments only does so because he is afraid of being laughed at.

Among what has been contemptuously referred to as the proletariat, in other words tourists who are content to spend their holidays walking in the valleys and over the lower slopes, I have met more genuine lovers of mountainous scenery than I have among mountaineers. Undoubtedly the physical act of climbing a mountain is a sport, yet to define mountaineering as a sport only is to omit incentive, cause, and effect, for the true mountaineer does not climb for the sake of physical exercise alone, but to establish some mental and spiritual contact with Nature. Therefore the sport of mountaineering, unlike most other sports, has a philosophical background, to neglect which is to neglect its *raison d'être.* In the same way a man does not go yachting merely for the sake of manoeuvring a yacht, he goes because he loves the sea and rejoices in the freedom of wide horizons.

Ruskin was right when he wrote that the beauty of mountains is best appreciated from the valleys. He might have said that beauty is better appreciated through in-action than through action. The mountaineer, who is interested in getting up and getting down a mountain as expeditiously as possible, and who in the matter of time and speed is concerned only with the competitive aspects of the sport, necessarily misses beauty. The true mountaineer, I affirm, that is the man who climbs mountains for spiritual as well as for physical reasons, is not concerned with haste except in the interests of safety, and likes to spend as many hours as possible on a mountain in order to contemplate the scenery. This is not to say that long and difficult climbs on which speed is essential are not part and parcel of the mountaineer's philosophy. They are a very necessary part because they provide a contrast as well as a test, and mountaineering is in the nature of a test between man and mountain. To enjoy mountains and mountaineering to the full a com-promise must be effected between the active and the passive make-up of a man. Ruskin did not get all he might have done out of mountains because he was content merely to contemplate them, but the mountaineer who rushes up and down mountains gets far less. To appreciate mountaineering to the full it is necessary correctly to assess the relative needs and merits of the physical, mental, and spiritual qualities, and he is a connoisseur of life who recognises this.

From the hamlet of Notre-Dame-de-la-Gorge, where the road ended, we proceeded on foot up a steep, roughly-cobbled path to the Chalets de Nant-Borrant. This was also the goal of the tourists in the motor-coach, and it was interesting to note the speed with which they walked. For our part we trudged slowly along and presently over-took them. They were all puffing heavily. It is a peculiarly distressing form of progression, this rushing and puffing uphill; not one person in a hundred knows how to climb with the minimum of effort. It is perfectly easy. Firstly, go slowly. Secondly, go steadily and do not stop, except when you want to for reasons of sightseeing. Thirdly, do not walk on the toes, but endeavour to place the whole foot on the ground. Fourthly, transfer the weight from foot to foot deliberately and rhythmically in a slow easy action devoid of any spring or jerking. Fifthly, take short steps. It is a case of the tortoise and the hare; you will be surprised how easily you overtake those who have passed you in the first place, arriving at your destination almost as fresh as you were when you started.

A pleasant path through cool woodlands took us uphill towards the Trélatête Hotel. The afternoon was overcast and oppressive, and the silent forest held a threat of storm. Whether on foot or on ski, there is something peculiarly enjoyable about ascending a path through a pine forest. Pines are restful trees, and the resinous smell that per-meates the still atmosphere beneath them is very soothing. A pine forest speaks and breathes of hills. To some people it is sombre and sad, full of furtive whisperings and dismal sighings. It is true there are occasions when it gathers to itself the quintessence of solemnity and gloom, but unlike some forests, it is seldom menacing and threatening. There is in it an atmosphere of peace and tranquillity.

When mounting through a pine forest the walker is scarcely conscious that he is gaining height except in terms of effort. He may mount for hours and see little, except occasional glimpses of distant hills between the branches. Then, and the transition is abrupt, the character of the forest changes. He sees through the dim aisles a brightness which is resolved as he climbs into blue sky. Then, suddenly, the trees thin out and he steps from the forest on to an alp, where a few outpost pines stand, gnarled weather-beaten trees, that embody in their heroic force the steadfastness and endurance of the hills. On the wiry turf of the alp, he pauses, and gazes outwards and downwards along the way he has come. The view is beautiful and dramatic. His vision swoops in an instant down green sheets of forest into a valley, and beyond it over range upon range of hills. For the first time he feels the cold breath of the snow on his cheek, a vital, exhilarating breeze. One stage of the way to the mountain-top is behind.

The Trélatête Hotel is situated a few yards above the tree-line on a grassy neck connecting a spur with the hillside. It is not a beautiful building and consists simply of a rectangular box, a dirty white in colour in which are inset numerous windows. The proprietress was a middle-aged woman, a typical French housewife, always working, always cleaning, always cooking and always good-natured. I take off my hat to the thrifty, hard-working, cheerful housewife of France. She is the mainstay, the prop, the backbone of that country. French Governments may come and go, there may be war and rumours of war, but the French housewife goes on for ever. She is the spirit of France.

We asked whether Englishmen often visited the hotel; her reply was, very seldom, but there was a Mr X, who ran the ski-ing course for English visitors; he was a *gentilhomme*, an altogether estimable gentleman. Did we know him? Had we met him? We had to admit that we had not, and felt that our stock was lowered in the eyes of Madame by our not being acquainted with so distinguished a personage. We excused ourselves by telling her that this was our first visit to the western end of the Mont Blanc range, that we thought it very beautiful, very interesting, that the hotel was admirably situated, etc. etc., which went some way towards counteracting our ignorance in the matter of Mr X. I take it that Mr X. is an *habitué* of this part of the world. Many who read this will have encountered the hotel *habitué*. I remember on one occasion visiting an hotel in a remote Scots village. There were two *habitués* there, which is an unusual circumstance. When I entered the lounge I saw them seated in state on either side of the fire, crusty old gentlemen who stayed there every summer for the fishing. There they sat, each in his own chair, and I shuddered inwardly to think what might have happened had I inadvertently sat in one or other of the chairs. They were entrenched behind *The*

Times, and were not on speaking terms, because each considered himself more of an *habitué* than the other; I could almost feel them glowering through the columns of print. As for me, I was the only other visitor, and because I was not a fisherman was beneath contempt.

Then there is the story of an elderly member of the Alpine Club who was an *habitué* of a certain hotel in the Valais. It was the unwritten law at that hotel that guests should not change into evening dress. For years this law had been obeyed and no one had dared to break it. But one day there came to that hotel a visitor so ignorant that on the evening of his arrival he assumed a dinner-jacket. He was preening himself in the lounge, apparently under the impression that he was the only gentleman present, when the *habitué* entered. He paused horror-struck, then giving the perpetrator of the outrage a pulverising glare, walked up to him, and said in a voice loud enough to be heard by everyone present: "I have to inform you, sir, that dinner-jackets are not worn in this hotel."

There were few guests at the Trélatête Hotel, and the *salle-à-manger* was forlorn and a trifle chilly. The dinner, however, was excellent, and the wine moderate in price, considering that it had to be carried on mule-back from the valley.

An overcast afternoon had turned into a sullen evening, and when we went to bed, in a clean and comfortable room, rain was falling heavily. It was still raining the following morning and continued in torrents all day.

We agreed that it meant quantities of snow higher up, and that our plans of traversing Mont Blanc, and making an ascent of the south side, had gone awry. I told Jim, with a sort of gloomy satisfaction, that my bad luck with the weather was stronger than his good luck, to which he replied with invincible optimism that perhaps, after all, his good luck might win through.

The Trélatête Hotel, like all mountain hotels, is ill-adapted for a stay in bad weather. There are no comfortable chairs, in which last respect the foreigner is more fortunate than the Englishman, inasmuch as he can sit for hours on end on a hard chair, long after the Englishman has been reduced to furtive writhings and wrigglings. To the mountaineer bad weather is worse than tedious; he sees his precious holiday slipping away, hour by hour, and day by day. He becomes restless, and crotchety. He reads, he writes, he has an occasional drink; at frequent intervals he consults the barometer, tapping the unfortunate instrument in an aggressive manner suggestive that it, and it alone, is responsible for the weather. Jim, a man of infinite resource, managed to unearth a set of draughts in which game we were joined by a cheerful young Frenchman, a university student who was spending his vacation wandering about the mountains. Finally when even fox and geese had palled, we were reduced to talking politics and discussing the possibilities of war occuring in the near future. An evil cloud was darkening over Europe. I had never been conscious of war-clouds on mountains, but I was aware of them then. It was not a fever like that of 1914 but a disease, a malignant growth, which mankind seemed unable to stem. A passionless, cold-blooded catastrophe was about to break on the world.

And all day long the rain poured down.

CHAPTER V

MONT TONDU

THE rain had ceased when we wakened next morning. Unwilling to waste another day, we decided to attempt the ascent of Mont Tondu, 10,485 feet, which stands at the westernmost extremity of the Mont Blanc range. It is not a long climb from the Trélatête Hotel, and we did not leave until eight o'clock. After the past five days of mountaineering inactivity, it was good to be on the move once more, and we both felt blithesome and gay as we mounted the path towards the Trélatête glacier. It was a pleasant introductory walk and the slopes were bright with flowers, shining in the luminous atmosphere. Our guide-book mentioned a *mauvais pas* which had to be crossed before reaching the glacier, but we did not see anything of the kind, and within half an hour of leaving the hotel were treading the ice of the latter.

The Trélatête glacier is less popular with tourists than the Bossons glacier or the Mer de Glace, but it is much frequented. Tourists who only visit the lowermost portions of Alpine glaciers must return sadly disillusioned, for, more often than not, they see the rubbish chutes of the mountains, a muddle of terminal moraines and melting, dirt-riddled ice, scenes not of pure ice and snow but of decay, ruin, and destruction. The lower part of the

Trélatête glacier has little to commend it in beauty or interest. The ice is dirty, so are the patches of snow in its hollows, and the slopes on either side are monotonous and shapeless. Sluggish mists contributed to this effect of dreariness, and it was a relief when between them we saw a glint of sunlight on the distant snows of the Aiguille des Glaciers.

Presently we came to an ice-fall, where the glacier flows over a steep step in its bed. We ascended this without difficulty, zigzagging between crevasses. As we did so, we noticed curious puffs of warm air seeming to emanate from the crevasses. I have noticed this before in the Alps and it is difficult to explain, seeing that air in crevasses should be cold.

The ice-fall was soon negotiated, and we emerged on to the almost level ice above it. Here snow was lying, and we paused to put on the rope. After crossing the level stretch, we mounted slopes of scree and snow to the tributary glacier which descends from the Col du Mont Tondu. Here we came to new snow which became progressively deeper as we ascended, so that presently we were sinking in well above the boot.

Ahead of us was Mont Tondu, an indeterminate-looking mountain. The obvious way to it was to continue up the glacier to the right of the col, but the slope here was steep and with much new snow on it might avalanche, so we decided to make for the col and follow the ridge from it to the summit.

It was monotonous treadmill-like work. Trudging uphill roped to a companion is less fatiguing than trudging uphill alone unless, of course, that companion has a pace entirely different from your own, when it is the reverse. The secret is to go slowly enough to allow the mind to detach itself from physical exertion, for it is a profound truism that when exertion is of such a nature as to occupy the mind to the exclusion of everything else, it is fatiguing. I do not mean, however, that the mountaineer should drift so far from his work as to be unready to meet a sudden emergency, such as his companion falling into a crevasse; he is not a good mountaineer who has not learned to react instinctively to sudden danger.

There is something very soothing about a long walk uphill, when heart and lungs are functioning with a minimum of effort and the pace is unhurried and rhythmical. The mind is disengaged, and free to contemplate with dispassionate detachment any subject it chooses, from metaphysics to the cut of a companion's trousers. Such contemplation, not being within the fixed time limits so often demanded by the exigencies of civilisation, prescribes a serenity in which time ceases to be of account. On many occasions I have walked up two thousand or three thousand feet of mountain-side and found myself at the top wondering how I got there. I seemed to have been transported thither by some magic carpet. The Easterner has translated in more practical fashion this detachment of the mind. He is able to exist without always doing something, or seeing something, or being amused, and he exists happily. To the Western mind, such browsing is ox-like, yet how simple and peaceful life in the West would be if we cultivated detachment.

I suppose that we should revert to the primitive in many respects because with the time factor ceasing to matter, the whole economic and social fabric would tend to disintegrate. Yet, it is certain that if peacefulness and happiness were the aims of humanity we would attain them.

We stood on the Col du Mont Tondu and behind us was a threadlike track curling down the snow-clad glacier. Except for that visible and outward evidence of our progression I should have suspected some satanic agency as responsible for our elevation.

It was warm and sunny on the col and we descended a few yards on the south side to a sloping ledge whence the new snow had melted, exposing rough warm rock. There we lunched. From our belvedere we looked down on grassy slopes to the west of the Col de la Seigne, a pass 8,245 feet high on the frontier between France and Italy. To emphasise this last fact there came from the Italian side of the pass the sound of gunfire, a vengeful growling which, amid the peacefulness of the hills, was as inappropriate as hiccoughs in a cathedral.

This would be a beautiful world were it not for the inclusion of man. What singular chance, what inter-positioning of Providence led to his inclusion? The sound of guns, the ridiculous little uniformed men swarming on both sides of the Col de la Seigne; was it to suckle these that Providence created the World? Why is it that everything in nature is appropriate except man; man the invader and destroyer of beauty, with his smoke, his smells, his noise, his nonsensical, illogical lust for killing his fellow men, his unquiet, his savagery, his defilement of nature and of beauty, and most of all his conceit and inappropriateness to the scene in which he has been cast? Has it ever occurred to philosophers that perhaps man is not indigenous to this planet, but arrived through some means from another planet where he was more appropriate, and that ever since he has been striving, without success, to adapt himself to conditions, which are fundamentally at variance with him, except in the matter of physical tolerance?

It was a delightful half-hour in the sun, and had it not been for my energetic companion, I might have remained there for the rest of the day. However, inexorable fate decreed that we must climb Mont Tondu, so languidly repacking our rucksacks, we set off up the ridge. It was mostly easy going, except for one steep place where the holds were concealed beneath new snow and some loose rock had to be negotiated with care.

Presently we came to a flat snowy shoulder on which some foolish person had erected a large cairn. Beyond this the ridge suddenly narrowed and became more interesting. It was never difficult, but the crest was sharp and the drop on either side formidable.

Much of the freshly-fallen snow had melted from the rocks and we scrambled leisurely along, until presently we came to the summit of the mountain. It was windless and warm there and the sun shone hotly through a blanketing mist. It was disappointing to have no view, and we decided to wait some time in the hopes of seeing one. My own experience of waiting on a mountain-top for a mist to clear usually resembles that of the man who stands watching an excavation being made in a road; nothing whatever happens except that the hole gets deeper. This occasion, however, was an exception, and we had not been seated for more than a few minutes when the mists parted abruptly and swept back like a curtain. In the gap thus formed Mont Blanc stood out radiant in its robes of freshly-fallen snow, a spectacle as beautiful as it was dramatic.

We spent an hour or more on the summit, and although there was little to be seen time passed like magic. Time usually seems to pass quickly in mountaineering. Human conception of time is based not so much on the movement of the earth round the sun as on personal interests, and if we separate these interests from the purely quantitative conception of time it is possible to glimpse dimly a fourth-dimensional state in which time as a measure of events and activity does not exist, and where events occur unaccompanied by and unrelated with that physical change which is essentially the bedrock of the human time factor; for time is a measure of life as we know it in this world. I have felt this very strongly on more than one occasion when climbing mountains; a sequence of events was in a curious way dissociated entirely from any sense of time. Thus, presupposing a survival of personality, it is possible to envisage dimly a state of existence which being related only to quality, and dissociated entirely from all quantitative conceptions as we know them here, is timeless. Thus a sequence of events is timeless, even though remaining a sequence because no quantitative conception exists in the personality which experiences it. It may be that sleep and dreams give us some inkling as to the nature of this state, for it is possible in a dream to break free from time and to be conscious only of a sequence of events which have no relation to time as a fixed quantity, whilst sleep, and for that matter unconsciousness, are timeless to the sleeper, and for this reason suggest a temporary dissociation of the spiritual and the physical, which is not memorable afterwards, when the association is resumed under the different order of conditions obtaining on this planet.

This may seem very far removed from the subject of this chapter, but I am sure that others who read this have had similar experiences with regard to time, not only when climbing mountains, but in many other walks of life, and it is interesting to delve into the subject, even if such delving leads only to suggestions and inferences of the vaguest nature.

We retired languidly along the ridge. On the snowy shoulder it occurred to us to see whether or not our previous determination to ascend by the ridge from the Col du Mont Tondu in preference to the glacier slopes was justified by the condition of the latter. So when we came to the rocks at the lower end of the shoulder we dislodged a boulder on to the slopes. Instantly the layer of new snow, perhaps a foot thick, began to slide. At first it was a small section a yard or two in width, but quickly the snow on either side began to slide too, forming an ever-widening wedge, so that in a matter of seconds hundreds of tons of snow were in motion.

At first the slide made a gentle serpent-like hissing, but as it increased in weight, volume, and speed the hissing was resolved into a harsher sound, as though a giant were sandpapering a piece of wood, and we saw the avalanche, for such it was, pour down the slopes with gathering momentum, and spread out in a mass of snow blocks three or four feet in depth on the glacier hundreds of feet lower.

It was an ordinary wet snow avalanche, and although we might well have escaped had we been overtaken by it when ascending from below, we might on the other hand have been overwhelmed and suffocated, for it is possible, as many disasters have proved, for a man to be buried and suffocated beneath an avalanche only a foot or so in depth owing to the manner in which snow consolidates when it comes to rest. For this reason the best chance of survival lies, not in trying to oppose an avalanche, or letting it knock you off your feet head downwards, but by endeavouring to keep on the surface by lying on the back and making swimming movements with the arms and the palms of the hands.

It was with great satisfaction that Jim and I watched the avalanche, for the mountaineer is only human, even if a trifle mad, and enjoys being proved right in his decisions. Thus we descended the ridge, pausing now and then to detach other slides, feeling unusually self-virtuous.

Back on the Col du Mont Tondu we halted for a rest and refreshment. The weather was still misty, but unquestionably on the mend, and we watched and photographed some effects of mist, light, and shadow, which dignified the little mountain we had just climbed into a giant of seemingly immeasurable height and remoteness. During the descent to the Trélatête glacier we indulged in the luxury of glissading, but because of crevasses deemed it advisable to retain the rope. Glissading on a rope closely resembles ski-ing on a rope. It is first of all necessary that the glissaders should be approximately equal in skill. Even so it often happens that one man sets off, and is proceeding at speed down the slope before the other man is properly under way, the result being that the rope tightens with a jerk which tugs the second man forward on to his nose. This halts the first man who waits resignedly for the second man. But the second man's blood is now up; he is out for revenge; with tremendous speed he shoots past the first man so that precisely the same thing happens in the reverse order.

Jim and I managed a trifle better than this, and slid down without misadventure until we came to a point where a diagonal descent had to be made. Here the snow petered out on to a small patch of ice above some stones and rough bare glacier. When I came to this my feet shot ungracefully from beneath me and I skidded on my back down the ice. There was no danger—I could have stopped myself easily enough on the stones—but Jim, very wisely, thought otherwise, and drove his axe into the snow above, halting me almost at once with an unpleasant jerk. He was right to do this, for there were crevasses below, and in mountaineering what may seem a joke at first may well have disastrous consequences.

Heavy mists still hung over the Trélatête glacier as we

descended, but on leaving the glacier we emerged into bright afternoon sunlight. For half an hour we remained seated on a flower-covered bank then strolled down to the hotel.

As an introduction to the western end of the Mont Blanc range, the ascent of Mont Tondu had proved admirable. We had seen enough to convince us that this region is beautiful and interesting. It now remained with the weather to determine whether or not we should be able to make other and finer ascents, including the traverse of Mont Blanc on which we had set our hearts, a descent into Italy, and a return over the south face of the mountain. There seemed every reason to suppose that it was improving; and the barometer, the most reliable prophet of all, and the most reviled, was rising, not abruptly and jerkily, but in that slow, steady, assured manner which presages a general improvement of weather conditions.

That evening the mists thinned and vanished, and the sun set peacefully behind the hills. We decided that another day of fine weather was necessary before setting off for the traverse of Mont Blanc, and that we would spend the morrow in making a second expedition from the Trélatête glacier.

When we went to bed the whole sky was brilliant with stars.

CHAPTER VI

THE TÊTE CARRÉE

WE were roused at dawn next morning. Other mountaineers staying at the hotel had been called long before, and had left for their climbs, but we saw no reason to start especially early for the Col Infranchissable, which was our first objective, and it was not until six o'clock that we packed the food provided by our hostess and set off for the climb.

In cold shadow we trudged up the Trélatête glacier and mounted the ice-fall, which a hard frost had rendered so slippery that we regretted not having provided ourselves with crampons.

Continuing up the glacier we presently overtook the first of the parties that had left before us, a man and a boy who were going very slowly and were already tired. The uppermost portion of the glacier provided pleasant walking over hard frozen snow, and we mounted rapidly, passing another party bound like ourselves for the Col Infranchissable.

Presently we emerged from shadow into sunlight and paused for a rest. It was a brilliantly clear morning, and the peaks of Dauphiné sixty miles distant stood out hard and clear with every detail distinct, the pinnacles on the ridge of the Meije, the graceful summit of the

Ecrins, and the narrow rift of the Coup de Sabre. The first halt on a snow-field in the sun is one of the best hours in mountaineering. Later in the day the sun pours down a furious glare, but early in the morning the sunlight is gentle and welcoming and in pleasant contrast with the numbing shadows. It reveals delicately, not harshly: long thin shadows and shining drifts of light, hollows and ripples, edges and ridges, the curves and volutes of the snow-field, the lacery and tracery of crevasses. Sunrise in the Alps is a slow awakening, not an abrupt and dramatic rousing as in the Tropics, and the mountaineer who treads the snows at this hour is conscious of some heritage of beauty, the purity of space, and elemental changeless things translated into visible and tangible form. Mountaineers are not the only ones to see beauty in snow. What is it that drives men to the polar regions? It is snow, the simplicity of snow, the sublimity of snow. What is it about the great elementals of the earth that appeal to men, the sky, the desert, the polar wastes, the mountains? It is only the fool who can look at snow and pronounce it to be nothing but frozen water.

The Col Infranchissable is situated at the head of the Trélatête glacier and to reach it involves nothing more than a walk. Intent on escaping from a chilly wind that poured through the gap, we mounted to a rock spur projecting from the north-west ridge of the Tête Carrée and there found a moderately sheltered place from which to enjoy the view. And the view surpassed all our expectations. It commands the whole of the south-west face of Mont Blanc, from the Brouillard ridge to the ridge on which we stood, on the main watershed of the range, which extends westwards from Mont Blanc to the Aiguille de Bionnassay, and thence to the Tête Carrée, the Aiguille de la Trélatête, and the Aiguille des Glaciers. From the Aiguille de Bionnassay the ridge bends south, and we looked across the south-west face of Mont Blanc. If the height of this great wall be taken from the Val Veni in Italy, it is some 11,000 feet, but from our position only the uppermost portion was visible, that above the Glacier de Miage Italian which is some 6,000 feet in height. This is without a doubt the most complicated mountain-side in the Alps, more intricate even than the east face of Monte Rosa. From our position we looked down to the Glacier de Miage Italian and, as we gazed at the tremendously steep stone-scarred couloirs that descend from the Col Infranchissable on this side, we marvelled at the temerity of the parties that have traversed the pass. It is true, of course, that seen from above a route always appears more formidable than it does when seen from below, but even so the ascent of the Col Infranchissable from the east must be one of exceptional difficulty and danger in all but the best conditions of snow and weather. Looking down the cliff at our feet we saw thousands of feet beneath the broken surface of the Miage glacier. High up, this glacier divides into three branches, all steep and tremendously shattered and broken. Between these are complicated rock ribs, and to the east of the easternmost branch rises the great Brouillard ridge which, with the even greater Pétéret ridge,

buttresses Mont Blanc to the south. So much for bald
detail, yet it is not detail with which the mountaineer
who sets eyes on this amazing view, is concerned. There
is too much to be seen, a veritable labyrinth of rock and
ice. I remember looking and wondering how climbers
manage to reach the Quintino Sella hut, then cross the
ice-fall to the east of it into the long couloir that runs up
to the Col Emile Rey from which the ascent of the
Brouillard ridge is made. Seen from the Col Infranchissable the whole route looks hopelessly impracticable, and
the view was an example of that mountaineering maxim
that until a route is actually attempted, always supposing that it is not positively and patently dangerous, it is
impossible to estimate its difficulties with any degree of
accuracy.

There is nothing serene about the view of the south
side of Mont Blanc except the summit of Mont Blanc
itself. The mountain-side before us was uneasy and
threatening, and in marked contrast with the snow-fields
over which we had ascended; it suggested not per-
manency but decay, ruin, and destruction. From our
lofty perch we could see every detail; processions of
lurching *séracs*, ice-swept couloirs with tongues of debris
at their feet, and everywhere the marks of avalanches.
And we could hear the processes of destruction in active
operation, even though the falls of stones and ice were
invisible to the eye, a clattering and growling rising on
occasion to a reverberating thunder that echoed and re-
echoed round the cirque. It was almost with relief that
the eye passed from this unbridled mountain savagery to

the south, where placid hills receded towards the snows of the Grivola, and the far distant heat hazes of the Italian plain.

From our vantage point the Aiguille de Bionnassay was in full view and we examined it with interest. There are few Alpine snow peaks to equal and none to exceed this mountain in beauty. From the Col Infranchissable it resembles the Ober Gabelhorn as seen from the Wellenkuppe; there are the same sweeping edges, the same elegant summit, the same superlative simplicity. The rocky section of the south ridge up which the route lies from the Durier hut on the Col de Miage was heavily plastered with snow, but another day of same hot sun we were now experiencing should put the mountain into safe condition.

Having assured ourselves on this point we turned our attention to the Tête Carrée. The mountain rises directly from the Col Infranchissable, and we had merely to follow the north-west ridge to gain the summit. This ridge was in a wintry state. The recent falls of snow had not accumulated to any depth, but had been blown by the wind to form plumes and cornices on the south-east side. The sun was shining almost directly down the ridge, and the fragile eaves and feathers of snow glowed with unearthly beauty.

The climb was not difficult. We began the ascent with some strenuous step-kicking on the west flank of the ridge, then mounted some rocks to a small shoulder. Above this the slope was icy enough to necessitate step-cutting. Jim made short work of this, and we ended the climb with a plug up soft snow to the roughly horizontal summit edge.

Apart from Mont Blanc, the view of which was essentially the same as that from the Col Infranchissable, we could now see the Aiguille de la Trélatête, the most popular peak of the district. A party was in the act of reaching the summit, and we could see their tracks on the long steep snow-slopes above the Trélatête glacier. We pondered on the possibility of continuing along the ridge from the Tête Carrée to the mountain, but decided against it on account of the steep slopes we should have to descend; the Aiguille de la Trélatête is decidedly not a peak to descend in the afternoon soon after a heavy snow-fall. The same considerations forced us to cut short our stay on the summit of the Tête Carrée and after a quarter of an hour we set off down.

Another party had climbed the peak by a different route from ours direct from the Trélatête glacier, and we followed their tracks. It was a steep but easy descent, but it was made disagreeable by soft snow and a sun-glare of withering, scorching intensity. In vain we searched for trickles of water, but in the end had to content ourselves with picking up handfuls of wet snow and squeezing out the moisture.

When at length, after a cautious descent, we reached the Trélatête glacier, we found that the hard frozen surface over which we had walked in the early morning had softened and refused to support our weight. The sun-glare here was worse if anything, and we ploughed down feeling like flies trapped in the globe of a powerful light. Thankfully we reached the side moraine and there imbibed copiously of a stream; how good was the feel of that cold pure water in our parched mouths!

I have one more memory of that climb; in some ways the most outstanding memory of all. It is that of a little shelf bright with thousands of creamy *Ranunculus Glacialis* with silken petals and golden stamens, a compact colony of plants in the midst of a stony desolation high up amid the permanent snows. It was an example of the tolerance of Nature, and of the unending adaptations that go to make this World. Life had breathed on that spot and, lo, it had been made beautiful.

Back at the Trélatête Hotel we met with a fellow member of the Alpine Club, Dr N. S. Finzi, and his Swiss guide, Franz Biener, and spent an enjoyable evening in their company. Franz Biener comes of a famous family of guides, and his is a name associated with many great ascents. There is no finer type of man than the first-class Alpine guide. First and foremost he loves the mountains, not as a means of livelihood but for themselves. He is quiet, gentle, and unassuming, for it is only inferior guides, or the money-grubbing type, who suffer from braggadocio and intolerance. There is much in common between the Alpine guide and the seaman; the serenity of their environment is reflected in their faces and in their character. The guide is a simple man, with a simple philosophy based on understanding, not cleverness. He has deep down within him an inarticulate faith in Providence, he is steadfast in purpose and a sense of responsibility is fundamental in his character. He pos-

THE AIGUILLE DE BIONNASSAY FROM THE COL INFRANCHISSABLE

sesses an instinct and an intuition for his work which comes only of long apprenticeship in mountain craft.

Only once have I climbed with a guide. That was during a search-party, and I was impressed, not only at the skill and speed with which he climbed, but at the margin of safety that in some indefinable way characterised his every movement. He who climbs with a first-rate Alpine guide not only feels safe, but *is* safe. The measure of the worth of mountaineering lies not only in accomplishment, but in the margin of safety over and above that accomplishment.

The weather was now set fair and we decided to traverse the Aiguille de Béranger and the Dôme de Miage to the Durier hut on the morrow, and the Aiguille de Bionnassay the following day to the Vallot hut. Then if the weather remained fair we would traverse Mont Blanc and descend to Courmayeur.

CHAPTER VII

THE AIGUILLE DE BÉRANGER AND THE DÔME DE MIAGE

A DISLIKE of an early start delayed our departure until 5.45 next morning. We had enjoyed our stay at the Trélatête Hotel, and were sorry to take leave of our hostess who, as a last *beau geste*, unhesitatingly accepted English money, together with the rate of exchange we quoted, although it was obvious that she knew nothing of the latter.

The sun was gilding the mountain-tops as we passed along the now familiar Trélatête glacier, and there was a promise of perfect weather in the sky, which was un-clouded, except for a few long-drawn filaments.

We were uncertain as to the point where the glacier is left in favour of the slopes of the Aiguille de Béranger. It often happens in such a case that two men take slightly different routes, each convinced that his particular route is the best. So it was in this instance, and it was with selfish satisfaction that I seated myself on a stone after a twenty minutes' scramble to await Jim, who had become involved in some awkward climbing up steep slabs. It is easy to preach against the evils of the competitive instinct in man, but however much a man may try to convince himself that he is above such feelings, if he is honest he will admit to a certain sensation of satisfaction as he watches a companion labouring up a hillside by a more difficult route than the one he has chosen. He may say, "Bad luck, old fellow," but what he really means is, "What a blithering idiot you were not to come up my way; it was a much better way than your wretched way."

The Aiguille de Béranger is one of the easiest peaks in the range of Mont Blanc, and one of the best viewpoints. Grass, gently inclined slabs, and patches of snow took us rapidly upwards. We halted for a meal below a snowy shoulder, assimilated the ubiquitous sardine, and toasted in the sun. The weather was perfect. Not a breath, not a whisper disturbed a profound quietude, and peaks and ranges rose unruffled by wind or cloud. The distant Dauphiné, with every detail distinct, glowed in the morning sunlight and opposite, across the Trélatête glacier, we could discern the marks of the avalanches we had detached on Mont Tondu, elongated smudges on the immaculate snow of that mountain.

It was evident that we were in for another grilling, and we smeared our already ravaged countenances with glacier cream. Sunburn can be a great leveller of persons. I have seen strong men, usually novices, scorn to smear themselves with cream. "What, put on that stuff, me!" they exclaim, as though it had been suggested that they should eat bread and milk in lieu of beef-steak, and they labour across the snow all day with an air of insufferable superiority, obviously contemptuous of "tenderskins". They return home triumphant, but with a red-hot countenance and a vague but dawning doubt at the back of their minds. The doubt becomes more pronounced that night as they feverishly toss and turn, with burning face and neck, unable to sleep a wink. They appear at the breakfast-table next morning short of temper and in colour resembling lobsters. But that is not all. Horror piles on horror. Their skin swells in bubbles until it resembles the peaks and craters of a lunar landscape. Then it cracks all over, even in the corners of the lips, so that a smile becomes an agony and talking an effort, until finally their countenances are reduced to a state of complete ruin. Then they growl at you with horrid imprecations (taking care not to open their mouths too wide) and say, "Why the blazes didn't you warn me about the sun?"

Continuing on our way we passed along a gently sloping snowy shoulder. The view from this is as beautiful as it is dramatic. For a few yards we looked down snow, then the eye passed from a gleaming edge, where the snow-slope bent out of sight, and in a single leap came to rest on hamlets, villages, and pasturelands 8,000 feet beneath. Such views are not so commonplace as might be imagined in the Alps. They may be enjoyed at their best from the northern wall of the Oberland, and the greatest charm when climbing, say the Guggi route on the Jungfrau, is to glance down on to forest-clad hills and meadows. Himalayan views are sometimes even more dramatic, and I remember well the amazing downward plunge of the eye from a height of 22,000 feet on Dunagiri into the Dhauli valley 15,000 feet lower.

It is possible to climb mountains without being especially conscious of the altitude when the climber is on peaks surrounded by glaciers, but he who climbs the Aiguille de Béranger in clear weather cannot fail to be impressed by his height and position, and the snow on which we walked seemed to be poised like some magic carpet in mid-air above the foot-hills.

The aeronaut has little impression of height because he is completely detached from the earth, whereas the occupant of a captive balloon is much more conscious of his position and altitude. Doubtless there are many who, if transported to such a position, would experience giddiness or sickness, accompanied perhaps by a desire to throw themselves over the edge. Yet, it is not justifiable to assume that looking down from a mountain is disagreeable because of a dislike of looking down from a tall building or a sea cliff. For me the last two experiences are distinctly unpleasant, and anyone who can gaze unmoved upon the sea from the edge of Beachy Head need have no qualms as to his reactions on the most sensational of Alpine precipices.

It was a glorious pathway up which we walked. The sun was warm without being fierce and scorching; it lit the snow until it shone like pure silver; it revealed every detail of the slopes, every fold, hummock, and ripple, and cast blue shadows filled with reflected opalescent light.

What an excellent thing it is to stand on a mountain, conscious that your muscles have carried you thither without the aid of any mechanical contrivance; to feel superlatively fit; to be clear of eye and head, and strong of leg and arm; to breathe deep breaths of keen cold air and in each breath discern the power and beauty of the

Universe; to know a contentment untrammelled by any anxiety, and a peace of mind and spirit which is true happiness.

The shoulder levelled out and we came to the foot of the final steep snow-slope which ends just below the summit of the mountain.

We climbed leisurely, but it was warm work nevertheless, for the sun was full on our backs, and we were glad to make across to some rocks and drink from a trickle of water.

Others had already ascended the peak, and as we refreshed ourselves we saw them descending the slope a few yards away. There were several parties, some with, and some without guides. Their descent was not an inspiring spectacle, as few of them had any notion of glissading; the more venturesome went head over heels down the slope and the less venturesome subsided on to their seats. Unquestionably the Alpine guide earns his pay, even on such an easy mountain as the Aiguille de Béranger, and our sympathy went out to the guides, who were not only denied a safe and easy glissade, but had, in addition, to restrain the antics of their charges, who even on that safest and easiest of snow-slopes were fully capable of hurting themselves.

The most striking spectacle of all was the descent of a woman who, having abandoned all hope of retaining her balance, was content to be lowered down on her back. In the pioneer days of mountaineering women wore skirts. Nowadays, and doubtless very sensibly, they wear trousers or breeches, but this does not alter the fact that the female form is in shape singularly ill adapted for the wearing of men's attire, and presents the most ludicrous appearance when clad in breeches. Trousers are a little better, but it must be a source of wonder to many that winter sports resorts are alluded to as "romantic" or potentially "romantic". It would be more logical to associate them with broken romances, for to the aesthetic or the romantically inclined there can be surely no more unromantic spectacle than that of a be-trousered woman tumbling about a snow-slope on a pair of ski. It is scarcely possible to picture a Romeo wooing a be-trousered Juliet on the snows of Mont Blanc or Mürren.

Twenty minutes later we sat sunning ourselves on the summit of the Aiguille de Béranger, devoutly thankful that we had arrived late enough to avoid sharing it with a crowd. As it was, the crowd had left tangible evidence behind it in the shape of sandwich papers, chocolate wrappings, and orange-peel. Such is the fate of the better-known and easily accessible viewpoints of the Alps.

We were not long by ourselves, for presently another party approached by the ridge which connects the Aiguille de Béranger with the Dôme de Miage. Accordingly, we continued on our way towards the latter peak, which we had to traverse in order to reach the Durier hut on the Col de Miage.

The descent to the col between the two mountains was over snow-covered rocks of little difficulty. Here we passed the party we had seen. They were all wearing crampons and for that reason were progressing with difficulty on the rocks. These adjuncts to climbing have become a fetish with a certain type of Continental climber. Whatever the nature of the terrain, whether hard snow, soft snow, snow-covered ice, or rocks, crampons are worn, and what is more are worn in many cases before experience has been gained of climbing in nailed boots. Hence there are many accidents directly attributable to climbing on ground where crampons are not only unsuitable but dangerous. Soft snow, which balls between the spikes, is always treacherous, whilst such snow when it conceals ice is nothing short of a death trap. Regarded as an adjunct to climbing, crampons are valuable, but as a substitute for the nailed boot they are a snare and a delusion.

As far as the col we met with soft snow, but it was apparent that the long steep slope leading up to the summit ridge of the Dôme de Miage was frozen hard. Here crampons would be of real service and we halted to strap them on.

The slope as anticipated was icy and we mounted rapidly in short zigzags dictated by its steepness and the necessity to ease our ankles, which had to be considerably flexed on account of the angle. It was a long slope ending below not on the col we had passed, but on the Glacier de la Frasse.

If I had to be killed by a fall on a mountain I should not choose a snow-slope ending in a precipice or ice cliffs; there would be too long an interval of anticipation. Yet there have been instances of climbers falling great distances down steep snow-slopes and escaping with their lives, though I have heard it said that if the slope is icy and rough it strips a man first of his clothes and then of his flesh, a process altogether too mediaeval in character to be contemplated with equanimity.

However, no such thoughts entered our minds as we stepped steadily up the snow, for it was impossible to entertain morbid thoughts on that day of bright sunlight and exhilarating activity.

At length the slope eased away and we trod soft snow, which continued without difficulty over a minor eminence to the summit of the Dôme de Miage.

So far so good, and having cautiously cast around for a possible cornice, we seated ourselves in the snow and lunched. We had not been long engaged thus when we were joined by another party, a Swiss and his guide, who approached from the opposite direction. It was a pleasant encounter, not only socially but gastronomically, as the Swiss generously insisted on giving us handfuls of prunes. "I do not need them," he said, "for I must go down. I should like to go to the Durier hut with you and climb the Aiguille de Bionnassay, but it is not possible; my wife awaits me." Then, in reply to further thanks on our part, he said, "After all it is good, is it not, to give and to share? It is the comradeship of the mountains, that matters."

He was right. "It is the comradeship of the mountains that matters." He spoke a profound truth. Laugh at mountaineers and mountaineering if you will, decry the dangers, stigmatise the risks as absurd and unnecessary, but remember that there is no sport which better promotes international friendships than mountaineering, for it is dissociated from those national rivalries and jealousies which so often prostitute other sports when transferred to the international arena or Olympiad. Mountaineering has its black sheep; it is capable of producing thoughtless and callous acts, but there is no sport so productive of that goodwill and unselfish co-operation, which all people of faith know must in the end triumph over the material greeds and frailties which are responsible for the unhappiness of man to-day. I hope our Swiss friend will read this; if so, he will say to himself, "Well, at all events, it was worth a few prunes!"

There was no immediate hurry, and for an hour or more we lounged at our ease on the summit. Curiously enough, I remember little of the view. In memory's eye I can see the Aiguille de la Trélatête across the Trélatête glacier, and dimly discern some small dots on it, two of which were probably Finzi and his guide. I can remember also the Aiguille de Bionnassay, now close at hand, and the summit of Mont Blanc with a smooth cloud capping it, a cloud neither of us fancied. Then there was a glimpse down to the fields of St Gervais and Sallanches. But what I remember best was the sun. The mountain world that day, and on succeeding days, was soaked in sunlight. There was sunshine everywhere, on the heights and in the depths, on the columns of afternoon cloud ranged over the valleys, on the warm red granite of Mont Blanc, on the ice, and on the snow. The mountains were celestial, brilliantly lit, superlatively calm. The sun shone through an atmosphere unbroken by any wind, and it was in this sun-drenched silence that our way lay then and on other days.

On such an occasion it is impossible to think of men in stuffy cities engaged in encompassing the ruin of other men. It was impossible to picture misery, to envisage the spectre of war on those sunlit heights. There is a lesson for all men to see, in the hills and in the stars above the hills, and in smaller things also, in trees and fields, streams and flowers. There is a great question-mark in the sunny heights, in the purity and beauty of snow, earth, and atmosphere. We talk of heaven, as though it were some place better than the World. Is not that an insult to the Creator of the World? There is a peace in Nature, a peace in which death seems trivial and meaningless, a transition in some evolutionary process of which man is an unending part. But why hasten death through strife and suffering? The true index of war is not death, it is the misery and suffering it creates, which renders man incapable of appreciating the beauty of his environment.

The traverse of the Dôme de Miage is a fine expedition. The route lies for the most part over snow and is devoid of difficulty, yet it is always interesting and the views are magnificent. From the summit we continued over some minor summits to the rocky point where the ridge bends almost at right angles and falls steeply to the Col de Miage. The climbing here was more difficult, and to descend the snow-covered rocks needed care. It was chilly on this sunless northern side of the peak and we were glad when, after a downward clamber of 1,000 feet, the ridge levelled out into the rudely horizontal crest of the col. We wondered where the Durier hut was, there being no tracks of previous climbers to guide us, but could see no sign of it. It was a long ridge and we passed over various snow edges and rocky bumps until the ground began to rise towards the Aiguille de Bionnassay. There was still no sign of the hut, and our guide-book, a German publication, was annoyingly vague as to its exact position. Then, suddenly, just as we were becoming really puzzled and despondent, we saw it perched on the rocky slopes that descend to the Glacier de Miage Français about one hundred feet below the crest of the col. Only one end was visible; the remainder being buried beneath an accumulation of snow.

We had to dig away a snowdrift with our ice axes before we could release the door. Inside we found a single room about twelve feet long and nine feet wide, three-quarters of the floor space being taken up by a bunk. The interior was filthy. The floor was covered with a black slush compounded of dirt and snow water that had seeped through the walls. It needed fortitude and determination to look under the bunk, where there reposed debris of all kinds, ranging from pieces of paper to mouldering scraps of food and verdigris-coated tins. The bunk was equipped with dirty straw palliasses, pillows greasy with the hair-oil of past visitors, and about fifteen blankets, some old, tattered and threadbare, some comparatively new and thick, but all exuding a smell suggestive that they had been employed for an indefinite period in the deepest and dampest dungeon of a mediaeval fortress.

The cooking arrangements were simplicity itself; there were none. It is true that a stove had once been installed, but what terrible fate had overtaken it we could only conjecture. At all events the remains of it red with rust stood pathetically against one wall of the hut, whilst on the floor lay a dejected-looking length of iron piping which had been intended originally to conduct the smoke into the open air.

Such was our abode for the night, and we could only pray that the weather would not change and confine us to it for a longer period. If it did we could certainly exist for some time on our own provisions, and on the scraps of bread left by former climbers, but we shuddered at the thought of this last, for the bread was green with age and as hard as granite. There was one thing in our favour; we had the hut to ourselves.

Fortunately we were able to economise our methylated spirit by collecting water that fell from the snow on the roof instead of having to melt snow. As economy in fuel is important it would be convenient to climbers if huts such as this were equipped with guttering and a pipe from which water could be collected. As it was, we had to employ a variety of receptacles to catch the desultory trickles.

The position of the Durier hut enables it to receive the whole of the afternoon sun, and we spent a pleasant hour or two outside, during which we took the opportunity to dry our socks, puttees, and boots. As we did so, we gazed down the broken rock face and shattered ice-falls that drop to the Glacier de Miage Français. The route up to the hut from this direction looked both difficult and dangerous, especially in view of the recently fallen snow that still cloaked the rocks, and we felt that our privacy was assured. In this last we were mistaken.

The sun was fast sinking when, to our astonishment, we heard a distant shout. Peering over the edge of the little shelf on which the hut stands we saw four climbers toiling up the snow-covered rocks. They seemed to be making heavy work of the climb, which was not to be wondered at considering the state of the mountain-side, and when they approached the rocks immediately below the hut we shouted down to ask them whether they would like the assistance of a rope over the last steep section. They refused this and presently arrived climbing unroped but evidently tired.

The party consisted of three Frenchmen, one young, one middle-aged, and one elderly, and a guide. The last named was a member of the old school. He did not wear the usual beret of the Chamoniards but a grey cloth cap. Like most guides, he was attired in a thick cloth suit, with coat, waistcoat, and drainpipe trousers. Alpine guides are for the most part intensely conservative in the matter of clothing and rely, not unreasonably, on their physical powers to withstand cold and exposure, yet it is an undeniable fact that two or three layers of knitted wool and a light windproof suit, weighing in all two or three pounds, are warmer than a broadcloth suit four times the weight. In support of this contention there are many instances of guides feeling a cold wind while their more sensibly clad charges proceeded in comfort.

He was a simple, friendly, unostentatious man, this guide, with a pink boyish complexion, blue eyes, and a moustache of imperialist dimensions, and his first thought on arriving at the hut was to provide for the comfort of his employers.

Our immediate reactions to the entry of the party were similar to those of any Englishman whose railway compartment is invaded by an excursionist family, but a friendly atmosphere was soon established. We had set about making the Frenchmen tea when we saw them labouring up the slopes, but water took a long time to heat over our spirit cooker and our visitors substituted a small primus which we were told to use whenever we liked, a graceful and generous act.

They had come, they told us, from St Gervais and, like us, intended to traverse the Aiguille de Bionnassay on the morrow, though, as they confessed, it was their first climb of the season and they were not yet in training.

An area approximately twelve feet in length by three feet in width, which represents roughly the floor space of the Durier hut, when occupied by six men needs managing, if there is not to be frustration and irritation, particularly as regards culinary matters. Thus, while the middle-aged Frenchman and I cooked, the remainder occupied the bunk. The sun was setting as I heated a stew consisting of soup powder, bread, and pieces of bully beef, and peering through the little window, which admitted a modicum of light into the box-like building, I saw the sky afire, and the northern ice face of the Dôme de Miage glowing like a tumbling torrent of purest gold.

Cooking operations and the enjoyment of an Alpine sunset are scarcely compatible, and I had the uneasy feeling that Jim was hungering for his stew, and that any inattention on my part in favour of the sunset, resulting in an upset of our saucepan, which was perilously perched on a small and decrepit table liable to be jolted at any moment, would be visited by the wrath it deserved.

The operation was successfully completed thanks to the primus cooker, and seated on the bunk we devoured with a feeling of gastronomical ecstasy a stew which was solid in all but name. "A grand stew, Frank," was Jim's verdict; it is a remark that I treasure.

Supper eaten, we prepared for bed. This involved some preliminary mathematics in the matter of blankets. Six men into fifteen blankets do not go, but my companion, a brilliant mathematician, solved the problem with the suggestion that each man should have two blankets and each pair of men one blanket.

Though an excellent sleeper as a general rule, I did not do myself justice that night. I lay awake and listened to a gradually rising crescendo of snores, punctuated at frequent intervals by violent upheavals and stifled groans from the younger of the Frenchmen, who fortunately was two removed from me: it seemed that in his dreams he suffered tortures, and more than once I was tempted to wake him and put him out of his misery. Meanwhile Jim, always a sound sleeper, gradually appropriated more and more of the communal blanket, until I found myself engaged in a tugging match to retain my share. I was tempted to expostulate, but he slumbered so peacefully that I did not have the heart to do so. In any event, I was reasonably warm, and lay comfortably enough, having become accustomed to the smell of the blankets, my head separated from the greasy odorous pillow by a spare sweater.

It was a quiet night, except for a vagrant wind soughing past the hut and occasionally, from the direction of the Dôme de Miage, the muffled growl of an ice avalanche. Through the narrow window, now laced with frost, I could see the glint of a star, and all about our small abode reigned the peace of the high mountains.

CHAPTER VIII

THE AIGUILLE DE BIONNASSAY

We were awakened by the Frenchmen getting up. It was 4 a.m., and there seemed no occasion to follow their example, as the guide-book time for the ascent of the Aiguille de Bionnassay from the Durier hut is four to six hours, and we did not wish to spoil the pleasure of the ascent by climbing in cold conditions. However, they were so slow that nearly an hour later when we rose there seemed no prospect of them starting.

It is disagreeable to prolong the agony of an early start in the Alps, and an hour sufficed for breakfast and climbing preparations. At six o'clock we sallied forth, just as the Frenchmen were strapping on their crampons, and set to work to climb the ridge.

The morning was clear and cold, and our crampons bit with comforting assurance into hard frozen snow. We mounted quickly and without difficulty, first of all up a broad snow-slope, then over a mixture of snow and rocks which presently thinned out into a sharp crest. This last brought us to a shoulder from which the ridge sprang up steeply in a rock edge defended in its lowermost portion by smooth slabs of formidable appearance.

The previous evening the guide had assured us that the best route lay to the west of the ridge crest via a snow-filled chimney, but this side of the ridge was out of the sun and the chimney was a cold, inhospitable-looking rift. If we traversed to the east over some slabby ribs we should reach snow which, to judge from the snow we had already climbed, should be in excellent condition; and our climb would be made in sunlight. It is true that this variation was unorthodox, and well removed from the usual route, but that made it all the better fun and we determined to attempt it.

From the shoulder a nearly horizontal traverse across snow brought us to the first of some slabby rock ribs, which we planned to cross diagonally. The rock was by no means firm, and climbing it in crampons was neither easy nor pleasant. It would have been better to have removed crampons, but this is not easy on steep ground, and in any event the rock climbing promised to be of short duration. To begin with, we made the mistake of keeping too high, and involved ourselves in considerable difficulties on the slabs. This was my fault; I was leading at the time, and I must have wasted a precious twenty minutes in what is best described as "messing about". Finally we crossed the first rib at a lower point, then traversed an incipient icy gully and another rib, after which we mounted at a steeper angle, until we saw a promising snow-slope above us to the right. We made for this slope; it was fully fifty degrees in angle, but we were relieved to find the snow in safe condition. There was no time to be lost as the slope was full in the sun, and would become impossibly dangerous in another hour or so, and we climbed at top speed.

The slope narrowed, and was finally strangled into a shallow chimney between rocks. So far, so good; except for the loss of time on the ribs at the beginning, we had made height quickly, and the conditions had been ideal for crampons. But now came ice. The hot sun of the past two days had melted the new snow on the rocks, water had trickled into the gully and there frozen during the night. Thump, thump. Later in the day the sound of an ice-axe pick meeting ice may become dull and monotonous, and a measure of weariness, but early in a climb, when the air is frosty and the sun warm, there is no more inspiring sound in the ear of a mountaineer.

We were soon up. Then came rocks and snow; there was some steep climbing, but nothing to hinder us unduly. The slope lifted at an ever-increasing angle, ending in a delicate little scroll of wind-turned snow, a small cornice on the south ridge close to the final snow-slope of the mountain.

Up and up we laboured, our crampon points driving well home. Now the cornice was immediately above us. A pause to flog it clear, and we stepped on to the narrow crest of the south ridge at a point well above the steep rocky section.

The snow was untrodden; the Frenchmen were below engaged in climbing the rocks. We hallo-ed and heard a distant response. A short pause to rest, and we continued towards the summit.

The way now was clear. We had to follow the snowy crest of the south ridge, then climb a final snow-slope which ended at the summit of the mountain.

It was a simple and beautiful finish to a mountain climb. The slope was concave in form, a parabola of unbroken snow lifting to a fragile crest, a celestial, wind-tossed roller frozen and motionless.

As we climbed I remember looking to the right and seeing Mont Blanc shining and serene in the morning sun, then glancing down to the left across the snowy wave to the meadows of St Gervais and Sallanches 10,000 feet beneath.

And so to the summit, a tent-like edge of snow, a summit almost as beautiful and dramatic as that of Nilgiri Parbat in the Garhwal Himalayas, which I remember as the *beau idéal* of mountain-tops. The Aiguille de Bionnassay was won.

We arrived there almost simultaneously with a party of two women and a guide. Our French friends were half an hour behind us and presently joined us. It was nine o'clock when we reached the summit, and I for one would gladly have spent the next two or three hours there. A long stay, however, was out of the question. One glance at the route we must follow to gain the Col de Bionnassay disclosed enormous cornices. These would force us to traverse the south-facing slope, on which the sun was shining so fiercely that it was only a matter of time before the snow softened on the underlying ice. The guide of the first party was fully alive to the danger and after pausing a few minutes left with his charges.

We waited until our French friends arrived, in order to photograph them, then set off down in the track of the other party. It was not long before we came up with them. The guide was taking no chances, and we realised directly we trod the slope that it was one demanding unremitting caution. A little earlier it would have been possible to have walked across it in crampons, but the brilliant sun had softened the snow, and beneath this, as already mentioned, was ice. It is on slopes of this nature that accidents are most likely to happen, for crampons, though valuable if used with circumspection, may easily become death-traps on the feet of the inexperienced. The climber must estimate where it is necessary to cut steps into the underlying ice. If there is any doubt that the snow will hold his foot *in situ* then he must cut steps; he must also remember to kick any balling snow away from his crampons every few steps. To the inexperienced such slopes often seem simplicity itself to climb or traverse, but it must be remembered that snow usually varies in depth and that, whereas it may be deep and comparatively firm on the ice for a few yards, the next few yards may be the reverse. For this reason the weight cannot safely be transferred to the front foot until it is certain that the snow is firm and deep enough to hold. The skill involved in crossing such slopes lies in knowing where, and where not, the snow is to be trusted, and the experience required to determine this is considerable.

We felt profoundly sorry for the guide. His was the unenviable task of conducting two women across a slope that had in it every element of treachery and danger. Had his charges been experienced mountaineers all would have been well, but it was obvious from the way they climbed that they were raw to the job. They carried their ice axes in their outside hands, and leant towards the slope clutching at it with their inside hands, while the rope drooped down between them in a melancholy loop. Had the woman last on the rope slipped, she would have slid some distance before the rope tightened on her companion who would inevitably have been dragged from her steps. Could the guide have held both when it was seldom possible for him to drive his ice axe into the slope for more than one-third of its length? I am certain he could not.

So impressed were Jim and I with the weakness of the party that we offered to rope on to them, which would have meant that the two women were between experienced companions, but this offer was curtly refused by the guide, possibly because he thought that we wanted to rope on to his party for our own safety and that our presence would further endanger it! It might surprise him to learn that we were extremely relieved at his refusal!

The cornices were some of the largest I have met with in the Alps, indeed so extensive that the leading party had difficulty in avoiding them. Meanwhile the snow became worse and worse as we descended, and we did not hesitate to enlarge the steps made by the guide. It was a relief when we came to some rocks and saw that little more of the ridge remained to be descended to the col. The guided party halted here and we went ahead thanking the guide for his steps as we passed him.

A few feet from the col the cornices petered out and we were able to tread the crest of the ridge, the whole way to that point having lain on the south slope. We were in need of a rest and food, and to escape a cutting north wind excavated a platform in the snow just below the ridge. We had been going hard, and it was pleasant to relax taut limbs in repose, whilst a few sardines slid down our throats with the greatest of ease.

As we ate, the first of the guided parties passed, but our French friends were a long way behind and were going laboriously and slowly.

Continuing on our way, we mounted a steep but easy snow ridge, passed over a subsidiary shoulder of the Dôme du Goûter, and joined the well-trodden Dôme route which various Italian parties were descending after climbing Mont Blanc.

Never before had I been on Mont Blanc in such perfect weather. We were overcome by laziness and the warmth of the sun, and easily succumbed to the temptation of a siesta. So hot was the sun that when we came to some rocks we had only to plaster a slab with snow to obtain a trickle and a drink. For a long while we sat and toasted. Even the cold north wind had died away and Mont Blanc dreamed, as I have never seen it dream before, under a gentian sky. So still was the atmosphere so silent the great mountain, there seemed something almost unreal in our situation. We stretched out our limbs and gazed languidly upon the tremendous prospect of dazzling snow, deep blue sky, woolly white clouds, and violet valleys. Such peacefulness as this inspires the question as to the reason for the interposition of quarrelsome man, into the beneficent scheme of Nature, and the thought of war, which, had we but known it, was only a few days' distant, seemed so absurd, so fantastic, so completely and utterly inappropriate as to be unbelievable. Why live in cities? Why not enjoy the sun and the air? Why not exist simply and happily without the need always to be amassing needless materials? Is it not better to see and feel the brown soil and be a part of living, growing things than ensconced amid dead bricks and mortar? Is not the soft grass better than the hard unsympathetic street? Is it not man's true heritage the scents of the earth, moist turf, a woodland after rain, new-mown hay on a June evening; to see beauty; flowers opening their petals, blue hills and horizons overhung with tall clouds. Why has progress, civilisation, religion, doomed mankind to enclosures and cities, where he must needs crowd into communities so closely set as to deprive him of the sight of a patch of grass or a glimpse of blue sky? This is the question mark of the age. If this is progress then God save man from it; if this is living then it is better to be dead; if this is what is meant by man being made in the image of God, then Hell is preferable to Heaven. We talk of war as though it were a misfortune. Modern war is mass suicide, the result of unhappiness and frustration which produce in their train greed and hatred, the product of an environment so artificial and complex that it foredooms happiness (which is the child of simplicity) in advance. Who are we with our factories, our "Black Country", our coal-mines, our grimy smoke-canopied cities, and our slums, to air our innocence and preach our virtuousness? War is like a disease that manifests itself on the skin, but it is not the skin that is wrong, it is the blood. Not until man reverts

to simple living in natural surrounding and gains contentment will he free himself from the germs of unhappiness
and frustration which produce the particular fever of
war.

It is perhaps curious that mountains should inspire such
thoughts, but a mountain is only one manifestation of
Nature. Mountains are simple things; they have not been
rendered into complex objects by the hand of man, they
are too big to be spoiled. Life in the mountains, or for that
matter in any wild place far from cities, teaches over and
over again that human beings to be happy need only bare
and simple necessities, and that directly this teaching is
lost, and necessities become associated with unnecessary
adjuncts, economic factors intrude which make for complexity, and ultimately for unhappiness and strife.

It was nothing but a walk to the Dôme du Goûter.
There was no need to hurry, and we lounged uphill
enjoying every step of the ascent. But slow as we were the
French party were slower still, and we presently came to
the conclusion that they were very tired.

The Dôme du Goûter shoulders the final peak of Mont
Blanc, and it is easy to understand how and why parties
lose their sense of direction in thick weather on its complicated slopes, but on this most brilliant of summer
afternoons not a breath of wind ruffled the immaculate
snows, and the many tragedies that have taken place
hereabouts seemed distant and remote.

From the Dôme du Goûter there is a descent of a few
yards, then an ascent of two or three hundred feet to the
Rochers Rouges, on which stands the Vallot observatory.

This is now used solely as a hut and recently the French Alpine Club constructed another hut close by, an all-metal building which gleams incongruously against the snows of Mont Blanc.

My memories of the Vallot hut are pleasant and unpleasant. I have had reason to bless it when descending late from Mont Blanc after a long climb up the south face of that mountain, yet its cold and dirty interior remains a disagreeable memory. To tourists ascending Mont Blanc by the ordinary route it is a longed-for halting place at which to have a hot drink and be comfortably sick. In this connection I recollect being aroused early one morning after a chilly night by a party consisting of two guides and a tourist. The last named was a tall, thin, lugubrious-looking man who, for some inscrutable reason, carried a thermometer attached to a ribbon round his neck. As he stood in the doorway, looking the picture of misery he managed to gulp out, "Bon jour, messieurs"—then he was violently ill.

Undoubtedly the tourist who assails Mont Blanc without some preliminary training is a brave man, for mountain sickness, which in the Alps is more often than not a product both of imperfect physical condition and altitude, is as bad or worse than sea sickness, perhaps worse, for in sea sickness the victim can lie down, whereas in mountaineering he has to keep on his legs.

Since those days a hut-keeper has been installed at the Vallot hut and home comforts may be enjoyed. We entered a warm little living-room with a stove at one end, and bunks at the other, to be welcomed by the guardian, a phlegmatic, broad-faced man, an ex-guide of Chamonix.

We were very thirsty and drank quantities of a pale coloured liquid re-heated for the occasion and described as tea, which, as we subsequently discovered, was regarded by the hut-keeper as being worth almost its weight in gold, for we were charged seven francs a cup and drank between us some ten cups in as many minutes.

Nevertheless, we were glad to have such comforts, and when it is considered that the Vallot hut is the highest building in Europe with the exception of the hut on the Italian summit of Monte Rosa, and that everything must be carried up to it on men's backs, the visitor must expect to be charged high prices.

It was late in the afternoon when our French friends arrived. They had altered their original intention of descending by the Aiguille du Goûter route, and leaving their guide to go down to St Gervais had struggled on to the Vallot hut. They were, all three of them, very nearly exhausted. The youngest man was the most, and the oldest man the least affected. It was impossible not to speculate as to what might have happened to them had the weather changed during the traverse of the Aiguille de Bionnassay. It is probable that had it done so and a blizzard developed Mont Blanc would have added to its long death-roll.

The evening was bitterly cold, for the Vallot hut is the recipient of every wind that blows, and a strong breeze tore past, finding its way under the door with a vicious whoo, and discovering various creaks and groans in the weather-beaten building. It denied to us the beauty of the sunset as it was impossible to remain outside for long, though I managed to take two photographs with half-frozen fingers.

Yet the evening sky promised good weather for the morrow. The sun set in a lake of gold, shot with green, saffron, and blue, behind the serrated summits of the Chaine des Aravis. Long belts of haze below, and fine-drawn tendrils of cloud above, were filled with splendid colours, so that earth and sky were suffused for a few minutes with light, and Mont Blanc seemed to float in luminescent space.

The hut was crowded, for others were present in addition to the three Frenchmen and ourselves. Fortunately plenty of blankets were forthcoming as the night was intensely cold and our boots froze hard, but any possibility of a restful sleep was sabotaged for me by the younger of the three Frenchmen. It was my misfortune to be next to him, and he was unable to keep still for two consecutive minutes. All night he was engaged in desperate combats with imaginary enemies, and entreaties and curses proving ineffectual, I was forced to resort first of all to nudgings, then to joggings, and finally to kickings, and while he was composing himself to a further nightmare, endeavour to snatch a few minutes' sleep myself.

CHAPTER IX

MONT BLANC AND THE BRENVA

I WAS thankful when dawn broke, and I informed Jim with an ill grace that he had been slumbering like a hog, but that I had had scarcely a wink, whereat he, in the manner of a man who has enjoyed a sound and refreshing sleep, was suitably sympathetic and commiserating.

At breakfast we had more tea at seven francs a cup, then, having thawed our boots over the stove and strapped on crampons, we paid a staggering bill and sallied forth on to the snows of Mont Blanc.

After the close, steamy interior of the hut the keen frosty air was wonderfully invigorating, and my grumpiness, consequent on a wretched night, soon vanished. The promise of a golden sunset had been fulfilled and Mont Blanc rose serene into a cloudless sky, yet it was no morning on which to linger and a bitter little breeze spurred us into activity.

Other parties from the Grands Mulets were arriving at the hut as we left, and we were thankful that we were first away, and did not have to shove and jostle our way to the summit through the hordes that were congregating to ascend to it.

At first we were thankful for gloves and balaclava

helmets, but we soon warmed up as we climbed, and were able to appreciate our surroundings.

It has been said that the traveller should make a point of witnessing two sights, the Taj Mahal by moonlight, and sunrise from Mont Blanc. I had some years previously witnessed the first of these and now had the privilege of witnessing the second. So much has been written by abler pens than mine about sunrise seen from Mont Blanc that I hesitate to enter the descriptive lists. That morning we saw to perfection the shadow of the mountain cast upon a sea of mist lying some thousands of feet beneath and extending westwards as far as the eye could see. We also experienced the same sensation of isolation and elevation so frequently commented on by former travellers without however, suffering from the disagreeable symptoms of mountain sickness which can ruin the aesthetic pleasure of ascending Mont Blanc.

The ascent of the mountain by the ordinary route from Chamonix has often been associated with the treadmill. Physically it is undoubtedly a wearisome affair, without any saving grace of climbing variety. The walker has merely to follow a deep groove worn in the snow by the feet of his predecessors and he is certain to arrive on the summit, unless he tires of this proceeding and wanders aside to fall into a crevasse, becomes sick or otherwise incapacitated, or decides to give up and go home, which is what I should do if I were a tourist. There is, however, much in the way of beauty to be noted. This beauty is perhaps not always perceptible when viewed in the company of a pair of guides whose sole object is to hustle their charge as expeditiously as possible to the summit and down again to Chamonix, in order that further employment may be obtained with the minimum of delay. Beauty and commercial bargains are uneasy bedfellows at the best of times; on a mountain they are positively murderous. But anyone who is content to spend a night at the Vallot hut, as we did, and lounge up to the summit next morning, can hardly fail to enjoy the experience. He will, if he has never before scaled a high mountain, see beauty previously undreamed of. It will be borne home to him that snow is not a white substance without form or void but the petrifaction of grace and purity, a celestial coverlet capable, like marble in the hands of a craftsman, of being moulded by sun and wind into delicate, fragile, and unearthly forms. Therefore, go slowly up Mont Blanc and see the day strengthen on the snow, watch the stealing shadows, the glowing high-lights; snow set brilliant against cobalt blue; snow in waves and ripples; snow in long gentle undulations; snow in serene plains and shining edges; snow in slopes, crests and cornices; snow in smooth lofting domes and steeply pointed spires. Watch how this snow sparkles and glitters as though strewn with diamonds, how it varies in shade, reflecting the tones of the sky, the gathering, dispersal, and passing of clouds. See how it moulds itself in heaven, matchlessly pure, infinitely tender in form and colour.

An hour's walking and we stood on the summit.

The view from the summit of Mont Blanc is notoriously unsatisfactory from an artistic standpoint. The Alps lie far below and the eye, ranging over a multitude of

THE SUMMIT RIDGE OF MONT BLANC

mountains and valleys, is totally unable to appreciate the
extent and magnificence of the panorama. The view
resembles that from an aeroplane; the earth is too remote,
too detached, too flattened; there are no outstanding
objects to provide foregrounds and middle distances to set
off depths and backgrounds, and height instead of being
a stimulus is a drug. Great mountains are best viewed
from below or, perhaps best of all, from points half-way
up them, whence depth and height are equally obvious,
each a complement and a help to the other.

Yet that morning it was possible to appreciate the
beauty of the view from the snowy crown of Europe.
The morning was calm, but now and then there was a
slight stirring of the atmosphere, a bitter little breath that
came and went, the merest hint of the deathly cold that
reigns wherever eternal snow has its being. All else was
light. The atmosphere was brilliant, the snow like light
liquefied and frozen; the sun poured light into the World
and we who stood on that high point were invested
and permeated with light.

Then there were clouds. The south was given over to
clouds ranged over the violet depths of the Italian valleys,
citadels of vapour apparently as solid and impermeable
as the snowy dome on which we stood, clouds in woolly
masses with blue chasms deep in their glowing folds,
bronze-coloured clouds in vast anvil-shaped wedges,
lifted beyond the blue ranges out of the far distant Plain of
Lombardy. And between these clouds, with their shining
domes and arches, their uplifted cupolas, airy minarets
and unsubstantial pillars, was the blue of the hills; and

higher still, above their topmost edges, dominating their furthest reaching tendrils and fingers, like a myriad upraised shields, gleamed the eternal snows.

Here was fantasy and reality, fantasy in the misty convolutions of the atmosphere suggestive of strange dreams, queer imaginings, and untranslatable phenomena; reality in the lift and loom of cold snow and hard rock.

We saw the Grivola and Paradiso, the well-remembered forms of Dauphiné and the serried ranks of the Graians, in the east the upjutting Matterhorn side by side with the glowing snows of Monte Rosa, and northwestwards the clustered summits of the Oberland.

And now I suppose that I had better admit that I am writing from memory. Did I really appreciate what I have tried to describe, or am I at this moment vicariously enjoying the view from the summit of Mont Blanc? I remember that I photographed Jim and that Jim photographed me, and that my photographic enthusiasm was aroused by the marvellous lighting effects, and in particular by the clouds. But supposing I had been given a pencil and paper and told to jot down my impressions there and then on the summit of Mont Blanc, what would I have written? I doubt if I would have written anything; my fingers were too cold; I had to stuff them into my pockets after taking photographs, and I remember that the returning circulation hurt abominably. What a miserable thing the human body is when it comes to enjoying a view from a high mountain. How it puffs and pants, how it aches and complains, how wretched it can be. The Tibetan philosophers declare that it is unnecessary to ascend Mount Everest when it can be climbed so easily in spirit, but there is an abysmal gulf between the Eastern philosophy of material and physical *laissez-faire* and the Western cult of material gain and physical experience. Possibly the desire to climb mountains arises from a desire to effect a compromise. If so, it is the most effective compromise I know, and it has this inestimable advantage; it enables the mountaineer to accumulate memories, and the outstanding power of memory lies in separating and eliminating the physically unpleasant from the mentally and spiritually inspiring. Thus in this book I am able to live again, and in a different manner, the experiences of my mountaineering holiday. On this basis the philosophy of a mountaineer should be that a spiritual and physical compromise makes for a well-balanced philosophy. Yet there are some to whom mountaineering spells only physical exercise, and who pass unseeing and uncomprehending the beauties of the hills. There has, for instance, been applied to the attempts to climb Mount Everest a stark materialism out of keeping with the idealistic nature of that enterprise, and it is impossible not to feel, however illogical it may seem in view of the bad luck with the weather that has so far dogged expeditions, that the mountain will not be climbed until it is approached in a different manner. To climb mountains safely and successfully it is necessary to possess something more than activity and skill; we must have what Mr Winthrop-Young terms the "feeling" for mountains, and this "feeling" has a spiritual rather than a material basis and significance.

Mountains, perhaps more than any other aspect of Nature except the sea, bring men into touch with those universal forces which in their summation men call God. On them we are able to review our physical selves and glimpse the hidden regions of the spirit. We are brought in some inexplicable manner into closer touch with the creative forces out of which we have been evolved, and the experience is refreshing and inspiring. It enables us to view and review the material aspects of life for what they are worth, and they appear small and ephemeral when seen in association with the grandeurs of the hills. Small wonder that the Tibetan on his windy plateau has few material ambitions as we plain-dwellers know them. To him a manufacturing district would be nothing short of a hell on earth. In the same way the mountaineer, freed for a time from life in a city, looks down on the plain and wonders why he and his fellow men congregate amid smoke and noise, and what lasting happiness is to be gained from the struggle to accrue materials other than the essentials of existence. He sees in the quest of unessential things a false measure of human progress, and his mind is filled with wonder that mankind should neglect the simple enjoyment of the fruits of the earth and the possibility of happiness and peace.

We had decided overnight to descend to the Torino hut by the Brenva route and the Col de la Fourche. The ascent of Mont Blanc from Italy via the Col de la Brenva is a classic climb which was immortalised by Mr A. E. W. Mason in his book *Running Water*; and it occurred to us that it would be an interesting route down Mont Blanc.

The descent from the summit of Mont Blanc to the Col de la Brenva, between Mont Blanc and Mont Maudit, is nothing but a walk down a slope of snow, which furious winds have carved into ripples and crusted "soup plates". The Brenva route terminates a little above the col, and shortly before reaching the latter we turned to the south towards the edge, where the gentle snows of Mont Blanc break away in a tremendous face, falling towards the Val Veni 10,000 feet beneath.

It was likely that the past days of good weather had been utilised by parties in ascending the Brenva route, and it was no surprise to us to see tracks. We followed these, first of all down easy snow, then over steepening slopes. The Brenva route once possessed a great reputation for extreme difficulty on account of the *séracs* that defend the exit on to the col, but for many years past they have given little trouble, and have yielded to frontal attack without the necessity of making a difficult and exposed traverse on ice as was sometimes the case. Thus, in 1927 when I climbed the Brenva, I remember nothing worse than a steep little wall of ice about twenty feet high at the top of the climb, though the slopes below the *séracs* are always long and steep, and when icy may tax severely the powers of a strong party. Even so, there are few great Alpine routes to equal the Brenva in grandeur and sublimity.

Soon we saw the tracks of our predecessors bend sharply round a corner and vanish beneath a line of ice cliffs. Before embarking on the traverse we paused to take a photograph. I have seen many beautiful and dramatic scenes among the mountains, but none to surpass the view we had that morning from the Brenva. The photograph I took gives no more than a hint of this. It shows in the foreground a wall of ice stippled in sunlight like the facets of some immense diamond, then the depths of the Aosta valley 12,000 feet lower. The cloudscape was, if possible, even more ethereally beautiful than that seen from the summit of Mont Blanc. Diaphanous frag-ments of mist swam in mid-air between us and the dim blue depths where Courmayeur lay, and in the back-ground huge cloud pillars were ranged along the hills and valleys with the ever lovely Grivola enthroned amidst their luminous folds.

The depths at our feet were impressive beyond descrip-tion. We were perched on the edge of a cloudy abyss which seemed almost to breathe up at us catching us coldly by the throat. In one downward glance, in one swift glimpse, there came to us the realisation of height and depth. Grandeur, beauty, exhilaration, even for one fleeting moment, terror, were concentrated in that down-ward plunge of the eye.

From snow we passed to ice, a parabolic, bowl-shaped slope of it which had to be crossed diagonally. It was as well that we wore crampons, for without them we should have had to cut many steps. It was no place in which to linger. The route passed along the base of an ice cliff fifty or more feet in height. It was clean-cut and firm, except in one place where a piece had partially detached itself

166

and hung in a menacing flake, a hundred tons or more in weight, athwart the route. Sooner or later it would fall and sweep the slope below with irresistible force and anyone who chanced to be in the way would be trodden out of existence like a beetle.

This is the kind of risk inseparable from mountaineering. Whether it be falling stones or ice the risk has sometimes to be accepted by the mountaineer. But it is not accepted rashly or heedlessly, for he is a fool who climbs heedless of risk. There is a subtle dividing-line in the matter of justifiable and unjustifiable risks. Climbs undertaken nowadays in the quest for new Alpine routes are often unjustifiable and outrage mountaineering practice and tradition. It behoves the mountaineer to distinguish between fair risks, which involve only a remote chance of accident, and unfair risks where there is a strong probability of disaster. It may be argued by non-mountaineers, "Why climb at all, there is an inevitable risk, the risk of falling, attached to the simplest ascent?" To this the mountaineer may reply, "Why venture on the roads of England, there is always the risk of meeting with an accident." This the non-mountaineer counters with, "But I must, it is necessary that I should take that risk."— "Well, then," retorts the mountaineer, "do without motor-cars; our ancestors lived comfortably enough without these death-dealing contrivances. You are prepared to take your risk in order to conform to civilisation with its unnecessary luxuries; you must, therefore, allow me to take my risk in pursuit of my unnecessary luxury of climbing a mountain."

The traverse brought us to an ice rib sloping steeply down to some rocks. Other parties have climbed these rocks, but the route on this occasion avoided them in favour of the slope to the west. This slope consisted of well-frozen snow, fully a foot in depth, resting on, and well adhering to, ice. There was a veritable staircase up it, made by parties who had ascended during the past two or three days, and though the angle was high we had only to walk down it, moving both together.

It was an altogether different occasion to my ascent in 1927. Then, the snow was thin on the ice and step-cutting was necessary on the uppermost portion of the slope, but now we descended with almost ridiculous ease, merely having to take care that we did not trip over our crampons, or allow their points to catch in our breeches or puttees.

As we descended we met two ascending parties of two men each. The first consisted of moderately experienced mountaineers, but the second, composed of two youths, was putting up a pitiable exhibition of mountaineering incompetency. As is usual in such cases the rope was a curse rather than a blessing, and merely ensured the death of both climbers in the event of a slip by either. They were evidently tired too, to judge from their slow and laborious progress, and we wondered how they would be going by the time they reached the top of the climb, or what would happen to them should the weather change for the worse.

At length we came to the commencement of the well-known ice ridge. This is the *bonne bouche* of the Brenva route, and the subject of some stirring descriptions by the pioneers. Yet, like the uppermost part of the climb, it seems to be easier than it used to be, and there is no record, as far as I know, of a party in recent years encountering a blade of ice so sharp as to necessitate an *à cheval* method of traversing it.

There was no urgent hurry and we paused for a rest and a bite of food. A glance at a watch disclosed that no more than one and a quarter hours had passed since we left the summit of Mont Blanc, of which less than one hour had been expended on the Brenva route itself.

Ours was a splendid breakfast place. Before us stretched the ice ridge a hundred yards in length and level like a tent ridge. Beyond it was the dark peak of the Aiguille de la Brenva with its slender pencil of rock, and beyond that the luminous depths of the Aosta valley in which silver-lit clouds floated lazily. As though to emphasise the fact that we were now in Italy, the sun blazed down with a new-found power, so much so that we decided not to prolong our halt unduly in case we should encounter soft wet snow.

The ice ridge was easy enough; at the same time it was exceedingly sharp and required a fine balance and steady nerves.

We were soon at the end of it. There I was surprised to find that the route, instead of continuing along the rocky ridge which falls to the Col Moore at the foot of the Brenva route, branched off down a snow rib to the right, and after descending a gully, traversed the mountain-side almost horizontally to the col.

In 1927 the route I had followed kept close to the ridge crest, so that here was a new invention which, as it was probably easier than the ridge, we decided to follow.

The snow was none too good on the initial rib, for already the fierce sun had eliminated all traces of the overnight frost and we had to keep a careful watch on the possibility of an avalanche occuring. After following it for perhaps a hundred feet the tracks bore to the left down steep snow to some rocks at the side of the gully. Neither of us fancied the snow, and we took every precaution when descending it. It proved safer than it looked, and we reached the rocks without misadventure. Here it was obvious that, while the parties we had passed had walked up the east side of the gully, then crossed it horizontally to the rocks with ease in crampons, the sun had already softened the thin layer of snow clinging to the ice. There was nothing for it but to cut steps. The work was rendered additionally unpleasant by the possibility of falling stones from the crumbling crags that overlooked the head of the gully. I was, therefore, delighted when Jim expressed a desire to go ahead and perform this onerous task; it appeared that he wanted some practice in step-cutting. I fear that from my demeanour he must have guessed the relief I felt at not having to labour and sweat in the sun, which now bore down on the mountain-side with a ferocious power, for I agreed with alacrity, belayed myself to an excellent spike of rock, sat down with a contented grunt, and cheerfully bade him go ahead with the job.

He did so, while I yielded myself up, while paying out the rope yard by yard, to that sloth and laziness which is especially pleasurable when the other fellow is doing all the hard work. At the same time I kept a sharp look-out for falling stones; but only one or two harmless pebbles slithered down the gully, and he was left uninterrupted to his task of step-cutting. So quick was he that I had scarcely time to make myself really comfortable, or remove sundry intrusive stones from beneath me, when he had accomplished the traverse and was cutting down the far side of the gully.

Inexorably the rope ran out until at length I had to call a reluctant halt and stir myself into sufficient activity to follow him down the steps he had made, a disagreeable descent as the ice was running with water.

This done, we bore round a corner out of the gully on to a long traverse of the mountain-side, substantially the same route as that followed by Professor T. Graham Brown and I, when we ascended the Brenva face of Mont Blanc in 1927 and 1928. It was comparatively easy going, and half an hour later we stood on the Col Moore at the foot of the Brenva route.

A steep little ice slope brought us down to the Brenva glacier. Except for the passage of the gully the descent had been accomplished with astonishing ease, so much so that my companion must have formed an erroneous impression as to the merits and difficulties of the route. The difficulty of a rock climb is easily assessed, but such assessment is not possible in the case of snow and ice climbs where conditions vary from year to year, and it would be rash to label the Brenva as anything but a great climb which may, under certain conditions of ice and snow, be easy, and may, under other conditions, be both difficult and dangerous. It is in their capacity to change from year to year, and even from day to day that the charm of such routes lies.

The walk across the head of the Brenva glacier to the ridge of the Tour Ronde was a sheer purgatory, for the sun blazed with relentless power into the snowy hollow between Mont Blanc and Mont Maudit, and the snow was so soft that at every step we sank in almost to the knees. A sorry anticlimax it seemed after our stroll down the upper slopes of the Brenva, and it was with relief that we gained the foot of the slopes leading up to the Col de la Fourche which we had to cross to the Glacier du Géant.

Neither of us fancied the ascent to the col. The snow was in reasonable condition, but the route brought us under a threatening cornice and the rocks hereabouts are disagreeably loose.

Of recent years numerous miniature huts have been built on the range of Mont Blanc for climbs inaccessible without bivouacking, and one constructed of iron now stands a few yards from the Col de la Fourche, semi-circular in shape like a Nissen hut, and capable of accommodating with reasonable comfort some four to six climbers. A party of two were in possession, one of them being Armand Charlet, the most enterprising and energetic of the younger generation of Chamonix guides. They were there with the object of ascending the

Brenva face of Mont Blanc on the morrow by the route made by Professor Graham Brown and myself in 1928.

An hour later, after a welcome drink of tea, we took our departure and having clambered up to the Col de la Fourche set off down the far side to the Glacier du Géant. Here, quite unexpectedly, we encountered the most difficult and strenuous climbing of the day, for the heat of the sun had turned the snow into running slush, and it was necessary to cut steps into the ice beneath for the greater part of the descent.

Once again Jim craved for some practice in step-cutting, and this time he got it in good measure. For my part, I remained happily ensconced on the crest of the col in the sun paying out the rope as he worked his way down. When the time came for me to follow I passed him and we descended rope-length by rope-length, taking advantage of sundry rocks as halting-places and belays for the rope, until we came to the lowermost section of the slope, where the route traversed the slope almost horizontally above a gaping bergschrund. At one point only was it possible to cross the schrund. Here a downward jump of ten or twelve feet, and a forward jump of seven or eight feet, had to be made. It was an exposed descent to the jumping-off point, and every step in the water-soaked ice had to be made anew. Jim did this, and to safeguard us both from an unpremeditated slide into the cavernous maw of the bergschrund, cut out a bollard of ice round which the rope could be securely passed, a neat piece of sculpture which evoked all my admiration.

Then he descended to the lip of the schrund, called for extra rope, and took a flying leap on to the lower lip whence he skidded down the slope below into soft snow. It was skilfully done, and when he had risen to his feet and brushed off the wet snow from his person, he ironically invited me to follow.

I did so. It was not a particularly difficult jump, but I have never been enamoured of such leaps; they produce momentarily a queasy feeling in the pit of the stomach similar to that sustained during the first moment in a descending lift, or the rapid fall of a ship into the trough of a wave. Even twelve feet seems a formidable height when viewed from above, and gravity an obnoxious thing in that moment or two of hesitation preparatory to making the leap. Yet when the leap is made and the landing achieved, then, of course, the leaper vows it is nothing.

Thenceforwards we had to endure the dullest and most fatiguing of plugs through soft wet snow over the Glacier du Géant, while our countenances were scorched and shrivelled by the afternoon sun, which was reflected with a dry, merciless intensity from the snow-field.

En route to the Col du Géant we met a party of some dozen Germans all bound for the bivouac hut on the Col de la Fourche. Hefty, sweating fellows they were, and we wondered what Charlet and his "Monsieur" would have to say when they appeared. A sardine tin would be sparsely populated compared with that bivouac box, and we wondered whether the unfortunate pair would come through the ordeal alive enough to deal with Mont Blanc on the morrow.

Near the Col du Géant we passed a disconsolate-looking Italian tourist who asked us whether we had seen a friend of his anywhere. We replied that we had not unless, as we endeavoured to explain in French, of which language the Italian understood a few words, he was among those present on the Brenva route, whereat our interrogator brightened visibly and declared with relief that perhaps he was.

This incident reminds me of a story I once heard. Two Germans set out from a certain German town for a climbing holiday in the Alps. During their first climb together one fell and was killed. The other, having assured himself that his companion was indeed dead, said to himself with true Teutonic philosophy, "Well, he is dead, poor Hans —I weep for him one tear." Then, having dried the tear, he continued, "Hans would not wish me to spoil my holiday by telling anyone that he is dead, and to have him carried down and buried very expensive will be. I will therefore continue with the holiday and climb all the mountains that he and I were going to climb."

He proceeded to do so and had a most successful and enjoyable time. Then he returned home. A few days later he was walking in the street when he was stopped by a friend who, after asking after his health, enquired as to the whereabouts of the missing Hans. "Hans?" said the climber. "Hans? Let me see now, Herr Gott, yes! Hans, poor Hans, he fell and was killed on that first mountain we climbed!"

The Col du Géant is the easiest pass across the range of Mont Blanc. A large hut-hotel is situated on the Italian side easily accessible from Courmayeur by a rough path, which avoids permanent snow. It is usually crowded with Italian tourists and climbers during the summer months, and we arrived to find it packed out. While waiting for beds, we had no option but to find a corner in the *salle-à-manger* and have a meal, a scarcely enjoyable function in view of the fact that our clothing had been soaked during the descent from the Col de la Fourche. However, the world assumed a brighter complexion after some soup, poached eggs, and a flask of Chianti, which last, coming after a heavy day, had the effect of making us so sleepy that we could scarcely muster up the energy to climb the stairs to the dormitory in which two beds were eventually reserved for us.

The night was not enjoyable. Some fifty or more persons of both sexes slept in the dormitory on beds arranged in tiers; the roof was low and a single window, a foot or two square, was totally inadequate as a ventilator. Furthermore, our underclothing was soaked, and the only way we could dry it was to sleep in it. We also suffered from an intense thirst, which, however, was slaked by my enterprising companion, who deftly insinuated himself through the narrow window and returned with a cupful of snow gathered from a drift. For the rest, we tossed and turned in an atmosphere which increased during the night to a pitch of tropicality which no one but an Italian could have endured without complaint. Altogether, it was a sorry climax to a grand day's mountaineering, and I remember lying in a clammy bath of vapour from my wet underclothing, vowing, as I have often vowed before, that I would avoid Alpine huts for the rest of my days.

CHAPTER X

THE ROCHEFORT RIDGE

WE rose early next morning in order to carry out an ascent that we had planned overnight. This was the Aiguille de Rochefort, a peak to the east of the Col du Géant and the Dent du Géant, and to approach it along the ridge connecting it with the Dent du Géant is a fine expedition involving the passage of an unusually sharp snow crest.

We breakfasted in an atmosphere stale with food and tobacco smoke, and it was a relief to step out into the frosty air.

The light grew rapidly as we trod the frozen snow of the Col du Géant, and we had not gone far before we halted to watch the light of the rising sun creep down from the summit dome of Mont Blanc to the precipices of the Brenva and the summits of the Pétéret ridge.

I have seen Mont Blanc from the neighbourhood of the Col du Géant on numerous occasions, and experience of its difficulties and intricacies has only served to consolidate the feeling of wonder I always have when gazing at the great mountain. Whether or not a view impresses the viewer depends on many factors. The beauty of a mountain view would seem to depend to a large extent upon the disposition of the main lines. Nature as a designer prefers elliptical lines to straight lines; the World is curved and so, if we are to believe Einstein, is the Universe itself. This is not to say that Nature is invariable in her preferences; she has erected the Dolomites, which to my mind are bizarre and picturesque, but not beautiful. But the beauty of the High Alps depends primarily on curves and the arrangement and grouping of the resulting forms. Eliminate the curves from the ridges of the Weisshorn and what remains? A simple pyramid, a poor substitute for that sublime mountain.

Mont Blanc, for all its complicated bulk, is a mountain on which curves predominate. It is also a mountain of many contrasts, and the beauty of the view from the Glacier du Géant depends on these as well as upon gracious contours. The whole extent of the mountain is embraced by the eye, from the meadows of Entrèves and the forests of the Val Veni to the final dome of pure snow 12,000 feet higher. In a single sweep the vision traverses the Pétéret ridge, the greatest of all Alpine ridges, first of all over the peak of the Aiguille Noire set darkly against tender blue hills, where Mont Blanc shakes itself loose of forest, meadow, and upland; then the angular teeth of the Dames Anglaises, which fill the gap between the Aiguille Noire and the Aiguille Blanche; then in another lift to the crest of the Aiguille Blanche with its two points linked by a graceful parabolic snow edge, followed by another and lesser drop to the Col de Pétéret; and finally a glorious sweep, beginning in rock and ending in unbroken snow, to the summit of Mont Blanc de Courmayeur and the supreme snowy cupola. But this is not all: the eye continues, travelling along a skyline of snow to the Col de la Brenva, climbing again to the sharp point of Mont Maudit, sinking yet again to the Col Maudit with its defending bastions of ice, to end its journey in the splintered towers of Mont Blanc du Tacul.

Is there another view in the Alps to surpass this in beauty and grandeur? The eye can scarcely comprehend the soaring peaks, the frozen torrents of ice, the avalanche-scarred gullies, the gleaming steeps constituting the mighty wall. Bewildered, it descends to find lodgment on the intervening ridge of the Tour Ronde, which separates the Glacier du Géant from the jumbled ice that laps against the Brenva face of Mont Blanc. It is a fine ridge yet it appears insignificant in contrast with Mont Blanc. Perhaps it ought not to be there; it conceals the torrential Brenva glacier, yet it provides a sense of scale which would otherwise be lacking in the vista. Lastly, and this is the loveliest contrast of all, comes the westernmost bay of the Glacier du Géant, a shining unbroken snow-field where the shadows of the bounding peaks grow and shrink, and silver-lit clouds pass in the arms of straying winds.

The view to the east is altogether different in character. Here there is a muddle of broken rocks on which is set, in defiance of all orthodox mountain architecture, the queer spike known as the Dent du Géant. It was a fitting name to bestow on this rock. There is nothing beautiful or elegant in the tooth of a giant, and there is nothing beautiful or elegant in this rust-coloured pinnacle: it is perhaps fortunate that the giant in question lost his other teeth and has only this one left with which to bite the clouds and sky. As with a Dolomite pinnacle, it is impossible not to feel that the Dent du Géant was accidental to the scheme of things; it is brutal, not graceful, and would have been better left out. Even as a scramble it would be no particular loss, as to climb it, it is only necessary to swarm up a series of fixed cables, though in fairness it must be stated that there is a first-rate route unattended by such abominations on the north face. However, there it is, and unless it falls the victim of an earthquake, or is blown up by Signor Mussolini, there it is likely to remain for some very considerable time.

Our route lay up broken rocks to the southern base of the tooth. It was on these lower rocks that the greatest guide of his generation, Emile Rey, fell and was killed when descending unroped; in addition broken heads are not unknown hereabouts, as the Dent du Géant is ascended every fine day by hordes of people and the rocks of its plinth are dangerously loose.

To gain the west ridge of the Aiguille de Rochefort it is only necessary to walk across a snow slope at the foot of the Dent du Géant. Here we strapped on crampons, then proceeded up frozen snow to the crest of the ridge.

Numerous parties had traversed the ridge during the past few days, and we followed a track which in places amounted to a deep furrow. Even so, the climb was in every way worthy of its considerable reputation. I have traversed more difficult Alpine snow ridges, the north ridge of the Bietschhorn for example, but I cannot recollect any to surpass the Rochefort in beauty and acuteness, added to which is the fact that it is several hundreds of yards in length, and maintains its sharpness for nine-tenths of the distance. We agreed that the ice ridge of the Brenva was not to be compared with it.

On a previous occasion I had retired defeated from the ridge because of a wind, but on this occasion scarcely a zephyr stirred, and we had merely to exercise continual caution with our crampons, so as to avoid catching their points in clothing or puttees when swinging the leg forward.

Traversing the ridge was an altogether delightful experience, and Blondin, engaged in his culinary operations in mid-air above Niagara, can scarcely have experienced a greater thrill than we.

For the most part we moved both together, but there were one or two places where the ridge was so thin and unstable, and our balance so delicate, that we deemed it advisable to move separately; there were places also where the crest was undermined by small cornices which the tracks of our predecessors did not always wholly avoid.

The ridge was by no means level; it lifted up and down in an irregular wavy fashion, and was broken near its easternmost end by sundry small rock towers. All who delight in snow climbing, all who love an airy edge, all who revel in the niceties of balance should visit the Rochefort ridge. The traverse was over far too soon, and we found ourselves beneath the culminating rocky tower of the Aiguille de Rochefort. What a wretched anti-climax this proved, a crumbling shaley ruin of a peak, a disagreeable curmudgeon of a summit which, except for the view, is worthless as a climb. A *via splendida* had ended in a *via dolorosa*.

A party of two, an Italian lady and her guide, were in front of us, and we waited while they descended, because of the stones they were unable to avoid dislodging. They halted to give us their opinion of the climb, and to enjoin caution on the treacherous rocks.

Having removed our crampons we tackled the rocks. They were not difficult, but certainly needed care because of their unstable nature; it is impossible to clean such rocks by removing the loose fragments because the rock underneath is equally unsound.

Twenty minutes later we were sunning ourselves on the summit of the Aiguille de Rochefort. The view was little different from the one we had enjoyed on the snow ridge, except that we now saw the Grandes Jorasses in the east. Parties were on the summit of the Dent du Géant, and the still morning was rendered hideous by triumphant cat-calls and other offensive noises in which the vulgar delight to indulge on the summit of a mountain.

There were two good reasons why we should not linger on the summit. Firstly, climbing on the loose rocks beneath the Dent du Géant in the company of the hordes descending from that peak would be both disagreeable and dangerous, and, secondly, we had previously decided to descend to Courmayeur with a view to traversing Mont Blanc by one or other of the routes on the south side of the mountain. Therefore, after a few minutes we set off down.

An hour later we were back at the Dent du Géant. I think that Jim had some idea of adding the peak to the day's bag, but he thought differently when he saw the queue waiting to ascend the fixed ropes, and heard the shouts and screams of the ascending and descending climbers. Of all Nature's works, mountains are least suited to human gregariousness, noise, and vulgarity, and we were thankful to leave the peak behind us and descend the lower rocks out of earshot.

On the way down we were afforded one of those spectacles of human foolishness and incompetence which are nowadays all too common on mountains. The route from the Glacier du Géant up the initial rocks was obvious; it could have been followed by a blind man, yet a belated ascending party had already missed it and had managed to get themselves into unnecessary difficulty and danger. For some inscrutable reason they had elected to climb not the rocks to the left of an introductory gully, which entail only a simple scramble, but the gully itself, which is a natural chute for falling stones. For a time we saw them labour up directly in the line of fire. Then they came to ice. This decided them to leave the gully in favour of the rocks to the right of it. To do this they had to cut a dozen or more steps in ice. The leader accomplished this somehow or other, but the steps were probably poor ones, for the second man slipped out of them and very nearly pulled his two companions with him. Had the party fallen they might not have hurt themselves; on the other hand, there was a fair-sized bergschrund at the foot of the slope waiting, as Professor Tyndall would have put it, for an erratic body. To us, as we rattled down the easy rocks on the other side of the gully, the procedure of the party appeared so foolish as to be almost beyond the range of criticism.

Half an hour later we were back at the Torino hut where we paid our bill, had our passports examined and stamped by the resident gendarme, a phlegmatic little fellow, attired in the uniform of an admiral, then set off to Courmayeur.

It is a fearsome experience to ascend from Courmayeur to the Col du Géant on a hot summer's day, but the descent is merely boring and annoying, and the path curvettes and zigzags down a hillside which, for ugliness and looseness, resembles a gigantic slag-heap. On the way down I stupidly managed to turn my foot on a stone and sprain my ankle. It happened in a moment and I cursed myself as every kind of an idiot as I slowly hobbled along, wondering disconsolately whether the damage would render our future plans inoperative.

There are, I understand, two treatments for a sprained ankle. One is to rest it and the other is to exercise it. I determined to persevere with the latter treatment. It was successful, though the ankle remained swollen and subsequently took two months to recover completely.

Once the tree line was reached the descent was delightful; there is no pleasanter mountaineering contrast than to exchange the scorching glare of the high snows for a cool resin-scented pine forest.

The shadows were lengthening as we emerged from the forest on to the meadows of the Val Ferret, but what should have been a pleasant stroll to Courmayeur was rendered horrible by innumerable motor-cars that hooted viciously at us, then, to add insult to injury, raised clouds of choking dust in our faces.

Courmayeur is a popular holiday resort, crowded out in July and August with Italian trippers, yet it contrives to maintain something which its opposite number, Chamonix, is fast losing, the atmosphere of the past. If civilisation included only amenities such as cleanliness, hygiene, good food, and comfortable accommodation all would be well, but unhappily civilisation to many people nowadays is synonymous with the motor-car and the aeroplane. The one brings its stink, noise, and dust to formerly peaceful Alpine valleys; the other renders hideous the quietness of the mountains impinging its brutal row on the ears of those who climb to escape for a time from the former. Is it too much to hope that some future generation of men will regard with disgust that horrible instrument of mental and physical torture, the internal-combustion engine which has brought so much unquiet and unhappiness to the world of to-day?

We had evidently arrived at the height of the Italian national holiday, and accommodation for the night was problematical; however, we managed to secure beds at the Hotel Savoia where I had formerly stayed. At first we were refused accommodation, but luckily the proprietor remembered me, and we were given beds in a large basement apartment in which a chauffeur occupied a third bed.

That evening at dinner we drank Asti Spumanti, which perhaps more than any Italian wine loses its flavour and bouquet when transferred to foreign climes; I have never met with a satisfactory Asti Spumanti in England.

For many mountaineers Courmayeur recalls pleasant memories. It would be difficult to imagine a greater climatic contrast than that between this village and the snows of Mont Blanc. The climber may fight his way down through a blizzard in the afternoon and spend the evening at his ease under the trees of an out-of-door café listening to an orchestra or dance band. In such abrupt and pleasant contrasts lies one of the charms of mountaineering.

Unhappily our appearance was scarcely appropriate to the fashionable company in which we found ourselves. We had achieved a bath, and had shaved with a razor borrowed from the "Boots" but, for the rest, we had only the clothes we stood up in, and they were already dilapidated by the strenuous climbing of the past fortnight; thus our appearance was a trifle unsavoury, and there were no other climbers present to provide the necessary moral support. We were made fully conscious of our sartorial shortcomings when the head waiter placed us at a table in the company of two English ladies who, if I may venture upon such a speculative statement, were occupied between their holidays with the teaching of the young. With the most honourable and politest of intentions I ventured upon a "Good evening" and accompanied this remark with a reference to the settled state of the weather. But my greeting was received with a disapproving pursing of lips, a non-committal sound, and a haughty glare which meant, as well as any glare can, "Who are you? I have never been introduced to you. I have no desire to know you. I don't like the look of you." In a word I was put thoroughly, conclusively, and convincingly in my place, so much so that for a few frozen moments it needed little imagination to replace my immediate environment with a suburban drawing-room complete with lace curtains, china cupboard, aspidistra, and goldfish in a bowl.

CHAPTER XI

THE GREAT SIDE OF MONT BLANC

OUR immediate plan was to ascend to the Gamba hut and climb Mont Blanc by either the Pétéret or the Innominata routes. Next morning, however, I felt far from well; I had contracted a chill, probably as a result of not changing my wet clothing on arrival at the Torino hut and sleeping in damp underclothing, and fits of shivering alternated with a burning fever, the whole being accompanied by a bursting head. This, together with a swollen and painful ankle, scarcely seemed a happy preliminary for an ascent of Mont Blanc. However, acting on the same principle already applied to my ankle, I told Jim that we would go up to the hut, and that the mountain air, the panacea of all ills, would soon oust the germs.

Accordingly, after collecting some provisions, and assuring ourselves at the same time that further food was to be obtained at the hut from the resident hut-keeper, we set off along a dusty road blaspheming the innumerable motors.

It was a relief to turn aside into the Val Veni, though even here we encountered many cars and had to keep a wary look-out. Such activity seemed unusual even in holiday time, but we realised, when we came to the first restaurant in the valley, that we had inadvertently strayed down to Courmayeur on the Italian equivalent of a bank holiday. At all events, the scene that met our eyes was the nearest approach to Hampstead Heath that I have witnessed in the Alps: there was everything appropriate to such an occasion from orange peel and sandwich papers to accordions and performing monkeys. And upon this scene, between the pines, shone the snows of Mont Blanc. Here was one answer to those who ponder on the whys and wherefores of successful dictatorships; the gregarious instincts of man, the mob that cannot divest itself of its mobbishness even in the presence of mountains and in the quiet sanctuaries of Nature.

This was not the only mob. There was another near the Hotel Purtud, a quieter and, to judge from the private motor-cars, more exclusive mob. We lunched at the hotel and afterwards decided to spend the night there on account of my chill, which made me feel unequal to the ascent to the Gamba hut. I fear this hiatus in our plan must have been irksome to Jim, but he generously made the suggestion in the first place, and expressed his enthusiasm for the spot. "Why climb every day," he said, "when there are pleasant places like this?"

The Purtud Hotel is indeed a pleasant place. It stands amidst meadows and pine forest on the floor of the Val Veni beneath the precipices of the Aiguille Noire de Pétéret, where the Pétéret ridge makes its first lift towards the distant summit of Mont Blanc. It narrowly escaped destruction from an enormous rock-fall when the crest of the Col de Pétéret, and a chunk of Mont Blanc de

Courmayeur itself, fell down in 1920 on to the Brenva glacier. So great was the weight and momentum of the avalanche that the torrent of rocks poured down the whole length of the glacier into the Val Veni, to the consternation of the populace of the district, who thought that Mont Blanc itself had fallen and that their last hour had come. Yet, by some miracle, no loss of life occurred and the rock blocks, many of them the size of houses, were halted, almost on the threshold of the hotel.

The holiday-makers all left that evening and we dined in comparative peace. In an attempt to stifle my chill I swallowed a large quantity of Chianti, and followed up the wine with some quinine provided by the management. It was a pleasant and effective treatment, except for the quinine, and next morning, in spite of a feverish night, I was sufficiently recovered to ascend to the Gamba hut.

It was a perfect morning when we set off. The dew-soaked pastures were laced with a filigree of shining cobwebs, and far above, light evanescent mists clung to the precipices of the Aiguille Noire, a happy augury of settled weather.

As we strolled up the valley we passed various military encampments, the tents being camouflaged and concealed in the pine forest in such a manner that it would be wellnigh impossible to spot them from the air. The Col de la Seigne at the head of the valley is an easy grass pass, but the cost of forcing it in either direction, even if this proved strategically practicable, would be prohibitive in men and munitions. Students of military history and tactics believe, not without reason, that in the event of war between France and Italy the former country would have a topographical advantage along the Alpine frontier, as the Lombard plain is more easily accessible from the water-shed of the Alps than the lowlands of France. It is probable that this consideration, coupled of course with the question of Mediterranean sea power, proved a decisive factor in favour of Italian neutrality at the outbreak of the present conflict.

Apart from these military eyesores, the walk along the Val Veni was delightful. The path led us through a pine forest, then over a wooden bridge spanning a glacier torrent, where we were accosted by an officer who was inquisitive as to our destination.

Leaving aside militarism there is something wonderfully restful about this fertile valley beneath the precipices of Mont Blanc. Even though I were transported thither by some magic agency I believe that I should know instinctively that I was in the presence of mountains. What is this "presence" which the sensitive so easily perceive in the neighbourhood of high mountains? Is it due to some atmospheric resonance imposed almost imperceptibly on the ear, the product of stream and precipice? Is it sun-warmed turf and the scent of pines permeated by refreshing draughts from the snows? Or is it something subtler, and less readily explainable, something perceptible only to the innermost consciousness? Do the hills bring us into closer and more evident touch with spiritual forces? Why did Christ go up on to a hill to pray and meditate? Was it simply a desire for mental calm, or did His elevation bring Him into closer touch with inspirational forces? Many men have asked themselves these questions; the answer lies in their own inexpressible feelings.

After a rest in the shade of the pines we set off up the open mountain-side with the fierce southern sun on our backs.

There is no deception about the path to the Gamba hut; it means to go uphill and does so with continuous effectiveness. Some distance below the hut it mounts steep rocks. When I last came this way it was necessary to climb these rocks, but now steel cables make it possible for any reasonably active person to visit the hut. This is a pity, for the Gamba hut is essentially a climbers' refuge, a starting-point for difficult routes, and tourists, especially Italian tourists with their habit of sitting up late and love of clamourous nights, destroy the rest of those who start off for their climbs in the early hours of the morning, and are an unmitigated nuisance.

A band of some dozen or more tourists, male and female, were just leaving the hut when we arrived, and it was with considerable thankfulness that we witnessed their departure. They had, as was only to be expected, left a considerable mess behind them, and the temporary absence of the hut-keeper, who had descended to the valley to procure fresh supplies of food, had led them into breaking into the locked kitchen and rifling the stores of food and wine.

Water is some distance from the hut, but by throwing snow from a near-by drift on to the sun-warmed roof we soon induced trickles and filled our saucepan preparatory to making tea. We were engaged in this when two parties of Germans, one numbering four climbers, and the other three, returned from a reconnaissance of the Pétéret and Innominata routes on Mont Blanc. They were all young fellows, and the leader of the latter party, who was a commander of Alpine troops, insisted on our sharing their food, and presented us with a quantity of biscuits and Pumpernickel which he assured us his party did not require. It was a generous action and we were grateful. These Germans were all fit, active young men, and their leader was of that strikingly handsome type that Germany so freely produces; a lean, sun-bronzed fellow with a hawk-like countenance and piercing blue eyes. If these were representative samples of the German youth of to-day, then it is one of the greatest tragedies the World has seen, that a political ideology, based on the Divine right of force and fatherland, should imbue such men with its vicious principles. In those young fellows, all ardent Nazis, yet patently wishful to be friends with us Englishmen, despite the poison assiduously pumped into them for years, we could sense something of the tragedy that was being enacted in Europe.

The rest of the afternoon we passed basking in the sun outside the hut, and when that beneficent orb, which we had come to regard almost as an institution, disappeared behind the Brouillard ridge, a warm glow on the cliffs of the Aiguille Noire de Pétéret assured us of a continuance of fair weather.

Meanwhile the hut-keeper arrived, a youth of some

twenty years, who was accompanied by his mother, a little old lady with a pippin-like face and a pair of shrewd bright black eyes. Both carried tremendous loads, and we marvelled at the strength and activity of the woman, who had borne upwards of fifty pounds on her back from the valley.

Great was their consternation when they saw the forced lock of the kitchen door and the rifled pantry, and it was interesting to note that, although we were automatically dismissed as possible malefactors, the Germans came in for some sharp questioning and had to exculpate themselves. However, it was soon made clear that the tourists were the culprits for, to do them justice, they had left some money behind as payment for the food and wine they had consumed. It was plain, however, that this did not go far towards mollifying the indignant hut-keeper and his mother, who could not reconcile themselves to the fact that the kitchen and living-room sacred to themselves had been broken into, and loud and voluble did they wax on the iniquities of tourists.

We dined well that evening off spaghetti soup, fresh veal chops, and vegetables. Afterwards we shared a fiasco of Chianti with the Germans, who told us that they had come from Germany by car, and were returning after ascending Mont Blanc because they had no money left and prices in Italy, particularly of petrol, were high. They planned to bivouac on the morrow and complete the climb via the Innominata route the following day.

Most of the parties who have climbed Mont Blanc by the Innominata route have bivouacked in the neighbourhood of the Pic Eccles, where the ridge separating the Fresnay and Brouillard glaciers abuts against the south face of Mont Blanc, but Jim and I were not enamoured of a bivouac; it is all very well to spend the night by a comfortable fire within the fuel line, but it is an altogether different matter to sit shivering at a height of 12,000 feet or more on Mont Blanc. We determined, therefore, to carry through the ascent in one day from the Gamba hut. The hut is situated at a height of about 8,000 feet and Mont Blanc is 15,810 feet; therefore some 8,000 feet had to be climbed, a long ascent for a single day's work over difficult ground. We considered it essential to arrive on the Col du Fresnay 12,000 feet, at dawn, and we decided to reconnoitre the route before attempting the climb.

The Germans recommended that instead of ascending the Brouillard glacier to the Col du Fresnay we should follow a route they had made during their reconnaissance. This was to ascend the Châtelet glacier for a short distance, then cross the rock ridge between it and the Brouillard glacier.

The weather was still as perfect as weather could be when we set off on our reconnaissance the next morning. Leisurely mounting the little Châtelet glacier, which lies directly above the hut, we came to tracks in some snow where the Germans had descended from the ridge. Any liking we may have entertained for their route in the first place soon evaporated on the disagreeable slopes of shale and loose rocks, which we had to climb in order to reach the ridge, and an additional unpleasantness was falling stones to which the lowermost part of the route is exposed.

Apart from these disadvantages the climb to the ridge was easy enough, and the descent on the far side to the Brouillard glacier proved only about fifty feet in height, the ridge being almost flush with the glacier on that side.

Once on the glacier we again followed the tracks of the Germans, but presently came to a point where they turned off to the right, and after mounting straight up, traversed horizontally the steep slopes above the glacier under the rocks of l'Innominata, the peak immediately to the south of the Col du Fresnay. There seemed no particular reason why a direct and easier route to the col should not be made through the *séracs* of the glacier, and I suggested to Jim that we should make one in preference to the Germans' route, which might be awkward to follow in the dark. Accordingly, we mounted the glacier, crossing numerous crevasses and threading our way between some formidable *séracs*.

The Brouillard and Fresnay glaciers bear witness to the steepness of the south side of Mont Blanc, and there are few Alpine glaciers to equal them in angle. They are both tremendously broken up, the ice-fall of the Fresnay glacier in particular being notorious among mountaineers for its complexity. It would be difficult to picture a scene more savage than that where the Brouillard glacier originates. The glacier begins its uneasy journey towards the pastures of the Val Veni from the foot of the final wall of Mont Blanc de Courmayeur, and is enclosed for the greater part of the way by the

Innominata and Brouillard ridges. In appearance it resembles a pavement of immensely thick marble blocks upheaved by earthquake, and on three sides, in sombre contrast with the dazzling disarray of shattered ice, huge precipices rise, a whispering gallery that echoes and re-echoes the cavernous thunder of falling ice as the unstable *séracs* lurch over to destruction. Here is Nature at her starkest and grandest. There is nothing gentle, except for the graceful snow-crest of the Col du Fresnay and the summit snow of Mont Blanc de Courmayeur set in high and serene detachment above its pillared precipices of red protogine. All else is unbridled savagery; the loom of precipice, the slow downward jerking glacier with its constant outbursts of titanic energy, the clattering of stone-falls, the roar of avalanches, the grinding split of gravity-tortured ice. It was long after the major routes on Mont Blanc had been climbed before mountaineers set foot hereabouts. Not until 1919 was the southern wall of Mont Blanc, between the Pétéret and Brouillard ridges, climbed by Messrs Courtauld and Oliver, with their guides, Adolphe and Henri Rey of Courmayeur, and Adolf Aufdenblatten of Switzerland. They bivouacked on the Col du Fresnay and next day reached the summit of Mont Blanc after a climb of eight hours. They were followed in 1921 by three famous Italian climbers, G. F. and G. B. Gugliermina and Francisco Ravelli, who made a slightly different route up the face. They bivouacked twice, the higher bivouac being on the precipice of Mont Blanc de Courmayeur, an exposed resting-place from which it would have been difficult or impossible to have retreated had the weather broken. Since 1921 the route has been followed by numerous parties, for the most part with guides.

In 1934 the climb was the scene of a tragedy. Two young British mountaineers, J. D. Hoyland and P. Wand of the Oxford University Mountaineering Club, attempted it. Hoyland, in particular, had shown great promise on the British crags, but he and his companion did not possess the requisite Alpine experience for an ascent of such magnitude. They were missing a month before they were found on the Fresnay glacier having fallen from the rocks immediately above the Col du Fresnay. To me fell the task of organising the search-party, when it was at length discovered that they had set off from the Gamba hut. The leading guide was Adolphe Rey and his quick eye discovered the extreme point of an ice-axe pick projecting from recently fallen snow. It was on ground so easy, it seemed impossible that a slip had occurred, but it had, and we followed the line of the fall down a couloir to the Fresnay glacier. I shall never forget the speed and energy with which Rey cut down and across a stone-swept ice-slope above a berg-schrund at the foot of the couloir. We were only just in time to escape disaster. Rey went first down a deep groove of polished ice worn out by falling stones that intersected the uppermost lip of the bergschrund. He jumped out of the groove on to some avalanche snow that choked the bergschrund and I followed, not a second too soon, as next moment the groove was swept by a cataract of stones.

It only remains to be said that the dangerous task of conveying the bodies down the ice-fall of the Fresnay glacier was carried out by a number of Courmayeur guides, two of whom were slightly injured by falling ice and stones.

In order to reach the Col du Fresnay we had to dodge between *séracs* and crevasses. The crevasses were abysmal and insecurely bridged with sun-softened snow, but it was all plain sailing except for one awkward passage, where an insecurely bridged rift had to be crossed, and lodgment effected on its uppermost lip, and presently, after plugging up a snow-slope, we stood on the col.

The ascent of 4,000 feet from the hut had taken only a little over three hours. Nothing was to be gained by continuing the climb, for the route towards the Pic Eccles was obvious, and we could scale the first two or three hundred feet of snow in the dark, if need be.

The day was windless and hot and we halted for a meal. It was an impressive situation, and savage precipices enclosed us except to the south where, beyond the sabre-like snow edge that sweeps up from the Col du Fresnay to the rocks of l'Innominata, hazy blue hills and the violet depths of the Val Veni showed in pleasant contrast.

The descent was unexpectedly easy. We discarded the Germans' route to the Châtelet glacier, and followed the Brouillard glacier. There were fewer crevasses in this than anticipated, in spite of its steepness, and we enjoyed some exhilarating glissades. A final jog down screes and boulders brought us back to the Gamba hut little over an

hour after leaving the col, well satisfied with our reconnaissance, and thoroughly convinced that the Innominata
route could be climbed in one day from the hut and that
a bivouac was unnecessary.

The Germans had all left before us that morning for
their bivouacs, one party of three being bound for the
Pic Eccles, and the other party of four for the Col de
Pétéret, and except for a couple of Italians we had the
hut to ourselves.

We spent the remainder of the day at our ease in the
sun. Experience has taught me that to fill every day of a
mountaineering holiday with strenuous climbing is a
mistake. Climbing, interesting and thrilling though it
may be, is best valued and enjoyed when measured
against periods of rest and inactivity. A thing I have
often noticed is that mountaineers who attach importance to an off day, not as a necessary rest but as something to be enjoyed for its own sake, like the mountains
better than those who regard mountaineering primarily
as a gymnastic exercise. Of course, if a man merely
wishes to climb mountains and has no other interest in
mountains there is nothing to be said, yet it is impossible
not to feel that there are many who enjoy mountaineering who are never able to appreciate the beauty of
mountains because of a notion that to get the most out
of their holiday they must climb all the time. Let me
declare at once that I am an essentially lazy mountaineer.
As a rule when I get to the top of a peak I find that I
have a great desire to rest there in the sun and admire
the view. Spending every hour of every day in scaling

8*

mountains has a drugging effect on my mind, and I no longer enjoy the beauty and peacefulness of the hills. An off day comes as a pleasant oasis in a desert of physical effort. It is then that the beauty of mountains is best perceived. To extract the best from mountaineering it is necessary to strike a balance between the physical and mental powers. And the same principle applies to life in general. Is not the present state of the World proof that mankind is unbalanced in this respect? Material matters, and the mental efforts necessary to foster and maintain them, have led to a neglect of those spiritual considerations on which happiness and peacefulness so largely depend. The man who climbs mountains continuously and energetically usually has no time or inclination to appreciate beauty; he is concerned only with the physical interpretations of mountaineering. Similarly, to rush through life, to be occupied always with material affairs, is to miss a happiness and a well-being that is man's spiritual birthright.

It was pleasant to spend the remainder of a sunny day on the turf of the alp where the hut stands. Dense clouds that had formed in the Val Veni nosed their way up the Brouillard and Fresnay glaciers, but they were harmless vapours and the sun declined in a clear sky. After life in a great city it is a queer experience to recline thus and watch clouds and mountains; there is something restful and soothing in the spectacle; the mind relapses into a half-waking, half-sleeping condition that has in it a quality seldom perceptible amid the rush and bustle of civilisation, a quality of oriental detachment and repose.

As the sun dropped towards the Brouillard ridge the clouds ceased to grow out of the valleys. Nature became quiescent and breathless as though awaiting some revelation. The breeze died away; an opalescent light pervaded the atmosphere, subtly separating the ranges with its luminous breadths. There was no sound save for the constant percussion of glacier streams.

As the sun sank, radiating great arrows of light, and casting the shadows of every pinnacle and minaret on the Brouillard ridge far across the dusky sky, the cold shadow tide swept upwards, yet long after it had passed I could feel warm fragrant breaths from the turf at my feet.

The Péteret ridge reddened and reddened until its details were merged into a single plane of light and colour: buttress, rib, and gully were no longer distinct; solidity was lost and the whole of Mont Blanc's greatest battlement was transformed into a glowing unsubstantial splendour hung like an auroral curtain in the deepening green of the evening sky.

Assured of good weather for the morrow we turned in early and slept an untroubled sleep, until shortly after midnight when the hut-keeper and his mother roused us.

Sleepy and glum we clambered down from the bunk. Meanwhile the hut-keeper had taken a glance out of the door. "Is it fine?" I asked him. "No, Monsieur," was the reply, "there is mist." This was bad news. Was the weather breaking? We went outside to look for ourselves. He had spoken the truth. Mist enwrapped the hut and the moonless night was pitch dark, only a few of the brighter stars being faintly discernible. Surely it was only a low mist? As long as the stars were not obscured by high cloud there was a prospect of fair weather. In any event there was no reason why we should not start. By the time we reached the Col du Fresnay the weather should be showing its hand, and we could always retreat from there safely in the event of a storm.

The hut-keeper's mother was particularly solicitous for our safety. "You will turn back if the weather is bad?" she begged us. We promised her that we would, and for my part it was a promise that I had every intention of keeping: I had been caught before by bad weather on the south side of Mont Blanc, on the Pétéret ridge, and it was an experience I have no wish to repeat. Mont Blanc may spare once, but to expect generosity a second time is asking too much.

Bowls of steaming coffee, bread, butter, and jam put new life into us, and at a quarter-past one we said good-bye to our kindly hosts and trudged out into the night.

The mist was thick and we were thankful that we had gone to some pains the day before to memorise the route over the boulder-strewn slopes between the hut and the Brouillard glacier. In addition, Jim had erected small cairns with pieces of paper in the top of them, and helped by our electric brooch lamps we lost no time in picking them out.

The night was ominously warm, but this was probably due to the blanketing mist and the latent heat of the rocks, which for the past fortnight had been absorbing the heat of the sun, for when we came to snow we found it hard frozen.

Our decision to mount by the Brouillard glacier, instead of by the short cut advocated by the Germans, proved the right one, and with crampons on our feet we made rapid progress.

As already mentioned, there is usually little pleasure to be derived from an early start in the Alps, yet on that occasion we enjoyed the trudge through the darkness. We were bound for a great climb, and were hoping to carry through in one day what normally takes two days; thus an early start was essential. Then, the way had been prepared to the Col du Fresnay, and no route-finding or temper-provoking contretemps were to be expected up that point; we had merely to go steadily ahead up well-frozen snow wearing crampons; and, lastly, there was no need to hurry; we could go slowly and economise energy for the more serious work of the day, thus giving the inner man, who had been disturbed from his digestive processes at an unconscionably early hour, time to adapt himself to the proceedings.

In such circumstances there is a sense of adventure which neither time nor custom can stale. The mind occupies itself with the strangest imaginings and fantasies. There is nothing to see but the little pool of light cast by the lamp, the moving feet and legs of your companion, if he chances to be in front of you, and the dark forms of the mountains reaching up into the stars. Time, as a quantity measurable in terms of ordinary civilised existence, simply ceases to exist, and fancy places all manner of interpretations on the adventure: an essay perhaps in search of some sleeping dragon, the surprise of a citadel, the rescue of an imprisoned damsel or some such commendable and exciting project.

The mist, as we anticipated, did not reach far above the hut, and for the greater part of the way we climbed beneath an unclouded star-filled sky. Though we progressed easily and, as it seemed, slowly, three hours sufficed for the climb to the Col du Fresnay.

Dawn was breaking as we trod the snowy crest of the col, and in the half-light the scene appeared inexpressibly dreary, so much so that I found it impossible to rid my mind of the grim purpose for which I had visited the col five years before. I said so to Jim, and I think he felt the same about it as I did, for he said, "Let's get on."

We disconnected our brooch lamps, which had served us so well, and mounted the snow ridge above the col, our crampons driving into steep icy snow. All went well for a time, and moving both together we made height quickly. As we did so the light increased behind the sinister-looking mass of the Aiguille Blanche de Pétéret, which loomed opposite to us across the tangled ice of the Fresnay glacier, and soon the rocky mass of Mont Blanc de Courmayeur ahead of us was tipped with gold by the rising sun. It was some time before the sun reached us, because of the intervening Pétéret ridge, but a sea of mist, which lay below extending southwards as far as the eye could see, was lit up in crest after crest and billow after billow. For much of the day this mist remained cloaking the valleys, and it added to our sense of height and isolation on the flanks of Mont Blanc.

Yet we had little time or inclination then to admire the march of the sun over mist and mountain; we were too much taken up with the details of the climbing, and the necessity to combat time which, on a climb of this nature, wings its way swallow-like through the day.

The ridge above the Col du Fresnay presently merged into a steep snow-slope which ended in its turn against the rocks of the Pic Eccles. Our guide-book described the route as going to the west in the direction of the Brouillard glacier, then up the rocks to the summit of the Pic Eccles. We accordingly made diagonally upwards in that direction. There was no sign of any track made by the Germans *en route* to their bivouac, but we continued hopefully to a corner, only to find ourselves on the edge of a sheer cliff falling to the glacier. At the same time the rocks immediately above us appeared unpromising, and it seemed unlikely that the route lay up them.

After a discussion we agreed that we must retrace our steps for a short distance. This we did, and after losing about a hundred feet of height turned upwards on to steep broken rocks. The climbing was not difficult, but it was sufficiently strenuous to make us realise that we were likely to encounter difficulties before reaching the summit of the Pic Eccles. These forebodings were fulfilled. We gained the south-west edge of the peak and continued over increasingly difficult rocks, until we came to a point less than one hundred feet from the summit, where further progress was barred by a wall of steep rock. It now appeared that had we gone to the right instead of to the left in the first place we would have encountered little difficulty; thus by following the directions of the guide-book we had involved ourselves in much unnecessary trouble.[1]

It was a sensational place where we stood. Immediately above us the rocks swept up in a vertical wall. To the left the cliff fell sheer to the Brouillard glacier, and to the right slabs slanted steeply towards the Fresnay glacier. The only way of avoiding the impasse appeared to lie in a flanking movement to the right, which meant a descent towards the Fresnay glacier, and an ascent to a point above the wall, and I suggested to Jim that he should hold me on the rope while I investigated the route. He did so, and I climbed down a shallow groove for about fifty feet, traversed horizontally out of it, turned an awkward corner, and climbed slabs of moderate difficulty, until I found myself directly above him. As he was now well held I called down to him that to save time he should climb the wall with the assistance of the rope. This he did. It was exceptionally strenuous climbing, but he accomplished it so skilfully that I gave him nothing more than a tight rope on the most difficult section of all, where he had to climb an overhanging crack by means of a "lay back" which,

[1] Capt. G. I. Finch has since informed me that his party avoided the Pic Eccles by traversing to the left a short distance from the Col du Fresnay on to the Brouillard glacier. It seems probable, therefore, that we, not the guide-book, were wrong, and that we made the mistake of attempting to traverse to the Brouillard glacier too high above the Col du Fresnay.

being interpreted, means that the weight of the body comes wholly on the hands and arms.

A few feet more of easy going and we stood on the summit of the Pic Eccles. The Germans had bivouacked on a small platform there and almost immediately we saw them. To our surprise they were only a short distance away on the far side of the Col Eccles which separates the Pic Eccles from the cliffs of Mont Blanc de Courmayeur: they must have left their bivouac not above half an hour before, probably on account of a cold night, and the necessity to warm themselves in the sun before undertaking difficult climbing, and we felt more than ever thankful that we had enjoyed a comfortable sleep in the Gamba hut in lieu of a chilly and uncomfortable bivouac. The sight of them made us feel generously disposed towards everyone and everything, and we decided to halt and have our second breakfast, as there seemed little likelihood of finding an equally comfortable resting-place on the great face ahead.

The time was now 7.30; the sun was well up above the Pétéret ridge, and scarcely a breath of wind disturbed a serene and perfect morning. The other party of Germans bound for the Pétéret ridge had bivouacked on the snow of the Col de Pétéret; they were still in cold shadow and were only just setting off for their climb. We could see their bivouac place, a scooped-out hole in the snow, protected from the wind by a circular wall of snow blocks. They must have had a wretched night.

So warm was the sun and so excellent the delicacies in our rucksacks that the next hour passed like magic. It was with regret that we tore our gaze away from the glorious panorama of cloud and mountain, and it was a shock to find that the minute hands of our watches had spun through a whole circle. I recollect a feeling of resignation, coupled with a distinct tiredness and disinclination to continue, as we swung our heavy rucksacks on to our backs and set off for the serious work of the day.

The snow ridge linking the Pic Eccles and the rocks of Mont Blanc de Courmayeur is an airy affair, a blade so sharp and narrow that we did not hesitate to employ an equestrian mode of advance.

We were now on the rocks of Mont Blanc de Courmayeur. The ridge from the Col Eccles continues up these for some distance, more as an edge than a ridge, then loses itself in the immense red cliffs that dominate the upper part of the mountain.

Above the col there was no great difficulty for the first hundred feet. Then the rocks steepened and we presently came to the foot of the greatest single difficulty of the climb. This is where the ridge abruptly rises in a step some sixty feet in height. The only way of scaling the obstacle is to climb a more or less vertical crack. The difficulty of the crack had already been made evident by the time the Germans had taken to climb it, and it was no surprise to us when we were confronted by a rift of unusually repulsive appearance.

For my part, I was thankful that my companion was in good form, for I had little inclination for gymnastics that day. He climbed in brilliant manner, without hesitation, without delay, and as actively as a cat. As I watched the patch in the seat of his breeches growing rapidly smaller and finally vanishing from sight I wished devoutly that I felt in better form for such work.

It was even as I suspected. When a cheerful shout came down inviting me to follow, my strength was entirely unequal to the task, my ankle rebelled at the strain imposed on it by anything in the nature of a wedging action, and my heart, which normally jogs along at a leisurely forty to fifty beats a minute, felt as though it were trying to burst from my chest. Altogether I was very glad of something better than the conventional tight rope above me; thankful indeed for some lusty pulls.

Winded and weak I at length arrived at the top of the crack, which in point of fact is more strenuous than difficult. My form was so poor that when I had at length recovered we discussed the situation. Jim was rightly doubtful as to whether I ought to continue and suggested an immediate retreat. I would have agreed with him had we been faced with continuously difficult rock climbing, but from what I had read about the climb the crack we had just scaled was the most strenuous portion of the route. Therefore, I told him that I was prepared to continue. The strange thing is that, although I continued to feel weak for the next hour, I later improved to such an extent that I felt stronger, as we neared the summit of Mont Blanc, than I did at the commencement of the climb, and was going as well as Jim.

Above the crack we bore slightly to the left. Some easy climbing for a few minutes brought us to another vertical rise in the ridge. This was not so difficult to surmount as the crack, as there was a sufficiency of holds, but it was strenuous going, and again I was glad that the rope was above and not below me.

We now came to a shoulder topped by a roughly horizontal snow edge. The situation of the climber here is amazing and we paused to take photographs. We looked along the gleaming snow then down into an abyss filled with glowing clouds from which rose the gleaming summits of the Grivola and Paradiso. To the left loomed the Aiguille Blanche de Pétéret, its immaculate snow summit linked to a secondary rock tower by a curving ice edge. It is through such glimpses, caught and registered by eye and brain in the heat and stress of a great climb, that the mountains best communicate their beauty and majesty to the climber. Memory in mountaineering is a capricious thing. Stupendous panoramas pass unheeded and unremembered, yet little glimpses of comparatively insignificant detail are caught and registered: the small window in the fleeing mist with its momentary view of shining snow; the dewy petals of an upland flower; the morning sun on a granite slab; a stream glinting out of smoke-blue depths. Smell also is a potent factor in assisting memory. What mountaineer is there who does not recollect some subtle odour? The curious, undefinable smell of a quickly forming mist; the warm breath of distant pastures and pine woods coming unexpectedly out of the ice-cold depths; the smell of moist turf and flowers on the edge of the moraine; the sulphurous cannonade of falling rocks. And in sounds: the hollow croak of a raven echoing across the cliff; the

whisper of an unexpected wind, the sudden reverbera-
tion of avalanche or thunder; the hiss of skidding ice
fragments; the harsh clattering of falling stones; the inti-
mate talk of a stream; some tone or inflexion in the voice
of a companion. These, and many other things besides,
may be caught and stored for no apparent reason in the
memory.

The shoulder we had reached juts from the precipices
of Mont Blanc de Courmayeur. No argument is possible
with these plaques of red protogine. Smooth and sheer
they lift into the blue, and not even the warm southern
sun can soften their austerity. The climber can no longer
advance; he must go right or left; he can only go left.
The rocks he must pass over at the foot of the precipice are in strange contrast to the firm protogine
above; they were loose and shaley and unpleasant to
tread, and demanded especial care and watchfulness because of the wet snow that partially concealed them.

The traverse brought us to a corner beyond which a
huge couloir fully fifty yards in width cuts into the
mountain-side, a natural rubbish shoot which empties the
stones from a wide range of cliffs over precipices on to
the Brouillard glacier. Courtauld and Oliver when they
discovered the Innominata route in 1919 crossed the
couloir and mounted by the rocks of the west side, but
the Gugliermina brothers in 1921 preferred the rocks
of the east side until the cliffs of Mont Blanc de Courmayeur forced them to cross the head of the couloir.

As we approached the corner we heard the clatter of
falling stones, and an instant later a volley of missiles

flew past, hitting the rocks and flying far out into space
with a vicious whirring. At the same moment we heard
voices and realised that we were closing up with the
Germans. They had decided to follow the Gugliermina
route, and there was nothing for it but to wait until
they ceased to dislodge stones, which was worse than
annoying as all our mountaineering instincts urged us to
climb as quickly as possible. As we waited we noted that
stones, other than those detached by the Germans, were
continually falling down the bed of the couloir, some in,
and others outside, a deep groove that had obviously
been worn in the ice by their predecessors.

Several minutes passed: presently stones ceased to hum
and whizz past the corner and we ventured out of cover.
Popping our heads round a rock we saw the Germans.
They were engrossed in climbing the steep slabs at the
side of the couloir. We realised at once that crossing the
latter was the crux of the climb. It was a difficult and
dangerous traverse, difficult because of its great steepness,
and dangerous because of its exposure to falling material.
And this material consisted not only of stones but of ice.
The night had been cold and huge icicles, yards in length
and as thick as a man's thigh, had formed on the precipices overlooking the couloir. Now under the influence
of the sun they were being detached from the rocks and
were falling like huge javelins sufficient in size and weight
to constitute a real danger.

Our first care was to climb to a safer position,
and we shouted up to the Germans a warning not to
dislodge stones. They obeyed, and a few minutes later

we were in comparative safety. Then we paused to watch the Germans.

They were as anxious as we to cross the couloir with the minimum of delay. At first sight it seemed that the best way of doing so was to make for some rocks about midway across, climb these, and complete the traverse where the couloir was narrower.

The leader of the German party was of the same opinion, and began to cut steps in the bed of the couloir. He did not get very far. Stone after stone was racing down the rift; they fell every few seconds and, apart from those that careered down the groove, there were others that swept the rocks he was making for. Furthermore, the couloir was wide at this point and its bed consisted of a thin layer of slushy snow resting on ice. The dangers were great, so great that to brave them was unjustifiable. The Germans soon realised this: the leader cut a dozen or so steps, then he halted, and after exchanging shouts with his companions retreated to the comparative safety of the slabs.

Both parties ought to have reached this section of the climb earlier. There was no excuse for delay in the case of the Germans; they had bivouacked and should have been hours ahead of us, yet they had left their bivouac too late and had climbed too slowly. Possibly, part of their trouble was that, like most German climbers, they were burdened with unnecessarily heavy rucksacks. They would have done better to have gone either lightly laden with little in the way of bivouac equipment, and carried through the climb with the utmost possible speed, or have taken elaborate equipment and bivouacked again. The Gugliermina brothers were exponents of the latter technique and bivouacked twice on the climb. Jim and I, however, prefer to travel light and fast, for apart from its rigours and discomforts, a bivouac in the High Alps asks a great deal of the weather.

The leader of the Germans now decided that the only course open to him was to continue on up the slabs and cross the couloir at its head where it was comparatively narrow, even though the traverse involved risk from the icicles pendant on the cliffs above.

There was nothing we could do but wait until the Germans had climbed the slabs and crossed the couloir: we had already lost well over an hour, and with the danger of falling stones and ice increasing every minute as the sun poured its heat on to the face, the delay was exasperating in the extreme.

Presently the slow-moving Germans reached the point where it was necessary to cross the couloir and we were able to advance. It is possible that the enforced rest had enabled me to recuperate my strength; at all events I was now as anxious as Jim for action and went ahead up the slabs.

As far as possible I followed the edge of the ice, keeping a sharp look-out for stones and falling icicles. Both were now raining from the cliffs into the couloir, and the prospect of having to cross the danger zone was not one to evoke enthusiasm.

There was one awkward bit where a projecting rock tongue forced us into climbing the slabs. Crampons are dangerous in such circumstances, for the reason that it is difficult to determine whether or not the foot is likely to slip: the closer the foot is to rocks the greater is the security.

As we approached the Germans they began to cross the couloir. The ice at that point was softer than it was lower down, and the leader cut steps quickly across to the rocks at the far side. He was followed by his two companions, who lost no time in crossing the danger zone. Soon they were all across, and we prepared to follow their example. At that time we were halted on the slabs, I being some fifty feet above Jim. There was little or no security owing to the absence of hitches for the rope, and we had had abundant evidence as to the continuous steepness and exposed nature of the climb. I was on poor holds and was preparing to take in the rope while Jim advanced when of a sudden there was a shout of "Vorsicht!" from the Germans and the swish of falling ice. Instinctively I ducked in my head. Next moment the mass of javelin-like icicles hit the rocks just above me, burst into fragments and swept past me. The larger fragments missed me but a few of the smaller rapped me sharply about the body. It was a nasty moment and a further hint, if any were needed, that the sooner we were out of harm's way the better.

Jim soon reached me and a minute or two later we were at the edge of the couloir, ready to cross in the steps cut by the Germans. The distance was not great, and our eighty-foot rope sufficed to cover it; thus there was no need for us both to be on the ice at the same time, and some measure of security was possible. The most dangerous section of the traverse was near the far end. There the steps crossed the mouth of a ferocious chimney cutting deeply into the cliff above which was choked with ice and formed a natural chute for stones which fell every few seconds into the main gully.

The non-mountaineering reader will suppose that crossing an ice- and stone-swept couloir is a nerve-racking business, but the fact is that dangers encountered on a mountain usually induce a curious fatalism far divorced from any sensation of physical fear. It is much more nerve-racking watching a companion cross a danger zone than to do so oneself. It is, however, quite another matter deliberately to follow a route where the dangers outstep a reasonable margin of safety. The man who climbs the Grépon runs the gauntlet of falling ice from a hanging glacier for a hundred yards, but experience has established this risk as a fair risk. On the other hand, the man who essays to climb the Eigerwand exposes himself to an unfair risk and lays himself open to a charge of recklessness. It is in undertaking unjustifiable climbs that fear is most likely to occur. I have never been so frightened in my life as when climbing the ice wall on Kangchenjunga, for I knew I was doing something that was unjustifiable and that outraged not only the traditions of mountaineering but Nature herself. It is difficult to explain what I intend by this last statement, but mountaineers will understand my meaning. There is in mountaineering some point at which Nature passes out of sympathy with the climber and becomes directly and uncompromisingly hostile to him. When a man feels this, and to the sensitive man it is very evident, it is time to look out or to turn back; a frontier has been crossed, a territory violated, and the penalty is likely to be heavy.

The crossing was soon made, and having safely established myself on the rocks, I called upon Jim to follow. He did so, while I kept watch on the beetling cliffs above, and in particular the threatening ice-charged chimney. Nothing fell, and a minute or so later we were reunited, feeling that the worst was behind us.

We found ourselves at the base of an ill-defined buttress, bounded on one side by the ice-filled chimney, and on the other by a wider and less formidable rift. The latter appeared climbable if need be, but its loose rocks contrasted unfavourably with the firmer rocks of the buttress.

After the slabs and ice of the couloir it was good to feel firm rough rocks, with a sufficiency of holds and belays to hand, and we mounted quickly in the wake of the Germans. The climbing as before was continuously steep; indeed, when we later reviewed the climb we agreed that our predominant impression was the exacting steepness of the face and the absence of ledges and resting-places; there was not one place where it was possible to halt in comfort between the point where the traverse into the couloir begins and the summit ridge of Mont Blanc de Courmayeur.

It was not long before we again overtook the Germans. They preferred to make to the left into the couloir already mentioned, while we continued up the rocks to the side, only traversing into the rift a few yards from the point where it ended. Owing to some loose rocks we waited until the Germans had climbed out of the couloir. Then we carefully crawled over some precariously poised blocks to the head of the latter. We came to a curious snow mass and squeezing round it found ourselves on the crest of a shallow col separating a projecting buttress from the main mountain-side. Above were slopes of rock and snow sweeping up to the crest of the Brouillard ridge, which leads without difficulty to the summit of Mont Blanc de Courmayeur. Route finding was virtually at an end; hard work alone separated us from the summit of Mont Blanc.

The Germans had halted on the col. There was no room for us, but as we passed they good-naturedly offered us some candied fruit, which we accepted gratefully as our mouths were unpleasantly parched.

A little higher we halted on some rocks. It was 2 p.m. Five and a half hours had elapsed since we left the Pic Eccles of which time an hour at least had been lost by the delays already narrated. However, there was plenty of time in hand; we anticipated no further great difficulties, and promised ourselves a comfortable night at the Grands Mulets; with luck, at Chamonix.

The ocean of mist, over which we had gazed at dawn, had risen, breaking up as it did so. Its steamy folds enwrapped us for a few minutes, then drew aside, disclosing a glimpse of toylike woods and pasturelands at an immense distance beneath. There was no wind, no movement, no sound; Mont Blanc was sunk in profound sleep this serene and peaceful afternoon.

We roused ourselves from our lethargy and turned once more to the work in hand. We were on a slope of perhaps forty-five degrees in angle. In its lowermost portion, immediately above the precipices we had just scaled, were incipient rocky ribs; higher, these merged into unbroken snow, which swept up uninterruptedly for some hundreds of feet to the crest of the Brouillard ridge.

Much depended on the state of the snow. All day the hot southern sun had blazed on it. We might have guessed it would be bad snow, and it proved to be in the worst possible condition, sodden through and through and in texture resembling a conglomeration of wet hail-stones. Worst of all, it rested on ice, and was ready to avalanche. The one thing in our favour was that it was so waterlogged that it tended to slide in streams rather than *en bloc*, though these streams, as is usual in the case of wet snow, widened as they descended gathering mass and momentum as they did so.

The slope was a perfect crampon trap. This is not to say that it was easier to climb without crampons, in point of fact crampons were an advantage, but that something more than ordinary care had to be exercised with crampons. The snow resting on the ice varied in depth from a few inches to about two feet. Where it was thin, step-cutting was obviously necessary, but where it was thicker it was not so obviously necessary. Yet the temptation to trust to the snow to hold the foot had to be rigorously resisted; the snow had to be cleared away and steps cut into the underlying ice. It is true that there were sections of the slope where the snow was deep enough and firm enough to mount without the need to cut steps, but for the greater part of the way step-cutting was essential.

The non-mountaineering reader may exclaim impatiently, "Why all this fuss? If there is any doubt why not cut steps all the way?" He must try to picture to himself the circumstances attendant on the problem. A long bout of step-cutting, when it comes after many hours hard work and thousands of feet of exacting mountaineering, demands determination as well as physical strength. Furthermore, time is of vital consequence. It is so easy to take a chance on a mountain; nine times out of ten the chance will come off, but the tenth time it will not. Most mountaineering accidents, and almost all crampon accidents, are due to the tenth chance. They are the result of trying to save time and energy, or simply because of impatience, the kind of impatience that is bred in an age of speed and impatience. Above all things, it is necessary to approach mountaineering patiently: never hurry for the sake of hurrying, never subordinate the mind to the fatigues of the body; practice always a detachment of mind in which chances, difficulties, and dangers are weighed as dispassionately as the scientist weighs chemicals on a knife-edge balance.

We shared in the work and hard work it proved. In some places the ice was soft and waterlogged, which meant that a larger step than usual had to be made; in other places, it was of that tough, tenacious quality often found on slopes at a great altitude, which face south and are exposed to extremes of temperature. We cut straight up the slope as this was safer than zigzagging or traversing in the avalanchy conditions. The slushy snow had to be cleared away before step-cutting was possible and streams of it went swishing down the slope on to our German friends, who stoically endured the bombardment.

It was weary work. When we were resting on the rocks the slope had seemed short and easy; half an hour's work would land us on the ridge; but it seemed to become longer and longer as we flogged and hacked our way up it. Meanwhile the sun beat down upon our backs with an intensity that deprived us of much of our energy, and I well remember how the salty sweat stung my eyes when my turn came to cut steps.

About half-way up we bore slightly to the right on to an ill-defined snowy rib. This was better; the air here seemed cooler and less stagnant. Up and up we cut with a constant serpent-like hissing of down-rushing snow in our ears. We should have felt some excitement as we neared the long-desired ridge, but I remember only a profound relief; that slope was too long and too exacting to foster either interest or excitement; it simply represented a job of gruelling work that had to be done.

Jim was in the lead as we approached the ridge. He was full of beans, swinging his axe with a ceaseless and untiring energy as skilfully as any guide. Hack, hack, swish, swish, the last step was made. He plunged his ice axe deep into the snow of the ridge. We were there.

Only an easy edge of rocks and snow separated us from the summit of Mont Blanc de Courmayeur.

We moved a few yards along the ridge, then paused to photograph the Germans as they mounted the rib. I believe that they were as thankful for our steps as we had been for theirs across the couloir. As we watched them it was brought home to us how steep was the slope; they were emerging from an abyss thousands of feet deep, and the first objects visible beyond them were the moraines of the Miage glacier, 9,000 feet lower.

We were in need of some more food, so we scrambled along the rocky crest of the ridge till we came to a ledge wide enough to sit upon in moderate comfort. There we halted for half an hour until a chill little wind drove us on again. The Germans meanwhile passed us, but we overtook them a little later on Mont Blanc de Courmayeur.

We enjoyed the climb to Mont Blanc. After the blazing sun and motionless air of the south face, the atmosphere on the summit snows seemed charged with vigour; indeed, so cold was the breeze that we were not again encouraged to halt.

As we neared the summit of Mont Blanc de Courmayeur we saw the tracks of the party which had climbed the Pétéret ridge. They had completed their climb several hours earlier which seems to point to the fact that of the two routes the Innominata is the harder.

At 6.30 p.m. we stood on the summit of Mont Blanc. The last tourist caravan had long since descended, and the declining sun cast long shadows across the wind-rippled snow. A thin cold breeze was blowing, a shrivelling little blast that did not invite more than a few moments' halt.

As an end to a great climb the summit of Mont Blanc is ideal. No difficult ground separates the climber from the Vallot hut and Chamonix, yet the highest mountain of the Alps is a worthy climax to one or other of the great climbs up its southern flanks. For all the hordes that tread it on a summer's day, for all the sandwich paper and orange-peel that desecrate its summit snows, there is an aloofness, a remoteness, and a serenity about the great mountain unequalled by any other Alpine peak. Mont Blanc is the King of Mountains, and, like a king, rises above small vulgarities.

I remember shuddering in the bitter cold while Jim manipulated his camera, I remember the golden sunlight, and a multitude of glowing clouds, dusky valleys and snowy mountain-tops. I remember a feeling of unreality; we did not tread mere snow, nor a high point of the earth; we seemed uplifted in space. Here were no intricate mechanisms, none of those material things with which men surround themselves; here was nothing false or shoddy, nothing mean or ugly, nothing complex or difficult to understand. Here was no strife, no pettiness, no malice, no uncharitableness. Here was beauty, and a superlative simplicity, a dome of glowing snow immobile in the firmament. Here dwelt the Spirit of Peace and the serenity of God.

Leisurely we made our way down the well-trodden ordinary route, past the Rocher de la Tournette and the Bosses du Dromadaire. The snow was molten, the western sky aflame with gorgeous lights, the depths on either hand profound wells of deepest purple; overhead the first stars shone like a dust of pearls; and all about this celestial path was the frigid silence of an Alpine evening.

It was a wretched anti-climax to arrive at the Vallot hut and find it full up with climbers. We were compelled to spend the night in the new structure where everything is metal except the blankets and pillows. This hut has double walls which are supposed to promote warmth but we found it icily cold; a night spent in a refrigerator at the North Pole could not have been less comfortable. The hut is entered through a trap door designed to keep out driven snow and this gives the inmate a feeling of imprisonment. The windows are of opaque glass and it is thus impossible to see any view or observe the weather. It is depressing as well as uncomfortable to sit on metal chairs, food eaten off a metal table is strangely un-appetising, and there is something cold and unsympathetic about a metal floor. In general, confinement to this hut suggests incarceration in a submarine, but without the latter's saving grace of warmth and creature comforts.

Fortunately sufficient blankets were available and we slept moderately well, but breakfast next morning and a struggle with frozen boots was a wretched experience.

In fairness to the designers it must be stated that the hut had not then been fully completed, but when it is, it is difficult to see how it will ever be anything but depressing.

Wood is a friendly, homely substance and metal is the reverse; nothing can alter this psychological fact.

The sun was shining brightly when we emerged from our steel box and set off down to Chamonix, yet there were signs that the weather was at last deteriorating and heavy, pillar-like cumulus clouds, with backings of lurid false cirrus were gathering in the west and north.

When we were presented with our bill at the old hut we found that we had not enough money to pay for our extravagances in the matter of tea the previous evening. However, among the parties which had arrived from the Grands Mulets, was an English lady who kindly loaned us one hundred francs.

Mont Blanc is pleasanter to descend than ascend by the ordinary route and its long snow-slopes are delightful to stroll down in the morning when the snow is hard frozen and the sun not too glaring and hot. Even the ordinary route is not entirely free from objective danger, and on the Grand Plateau we came on the debris of an ice avalanche covering the track for fully one hundred yards, which had fallen from the *séracs* of the Dôme du Goûter. There is no need for the route to keep close to the Dôme du Goûter, but the Chamonix guides are nothing if not conservative, and prefer the remote risk of an avalanche to making a divergence, which would avoid the principal danger zone, at the expense of a few extra minutes of walking.

It was a charming descent. Before us were the smoke-blue depths of the Chamonix valley, and hills deeply shadowed with growing thunderclouds. We met with various ascending parties, among them a solitary climber who seemed already tired. We passed the Grands Mulets and thought of the pioneers who had slept there before embarking upon the great adventure of climbing Mont Blanc with their cohorts of peasants, their enormous quantities of meat and drink, and their perpetual fear of mountain sickness. To them it must have seemed a far greater adventure to tramp up the glacier to the summit, than it does for the climber of to-day to scale the southern precipices of the mountain. Is modern life tending to make men blasé in the search for adventure? What will happen when every square mile has been explored and mapped, when every Andean and Himalayan summit has been trodden, and the World, in terms of speedy travel, reduced to the dimensions of an English county? Will man's adventurous instinct and his virility find sufficient scope and variety of experience in following where others have trodden, or will he seek new worlds to conquer in interplanetary space?

There is little more to relate. We trudged down the Bossons glacier, zigzagged through the glittering *séracs*, hurried beneath the stone-swept cliffs of the Aiguille de Midi, drank beer at the Pierre Pointue and descended lazily into the Chamonix valley by the *téléférique*.

We lunched late at Chamonix, and as we did so the clouds thickened and thickened on Mont Blanc. Thunder began to growl. The weather was breaking. We had a day or two of our holiday left, but why wait? It would be a sorry anti-climax to struggle up some peak in the teeth of bad weather. Might it not efface the memories

of the past glorious fortnight? It would have been in-
artistic, a careless daub smeared on a picture of limpid
beauty. That evening in sullen ominous weather we set
off for England. Our mountaineering holiday had ended.

A few days later Europe was at war.

SOME BLACK JACKET BOOKS